Praise for *The Christian Mama's Guide to Baby's First Year*

Wish you had a mentor to walk with you through that first year of motherhood? Well, now you do! Erin shares a hope-filled, come-along-side-you guide for knowing how to handle the 24/7 details of living—and succeeding—with baby. Covering everything from nursing to diapering to medical issues and more, Erin tackles it all, but with a biblical view of God's wonderful plan for parenting. She even provides a daddy-to-daddy guide to help him on the journey. Be sure to start the trip with this valuable guide!

—Susan Mathis, Best-selling Author and
Founding Editor of *Thriving Family* magazine

Erin MacPherson is the best friend you've always wanted—witty, wise, informative, and godly. In her Christian Mama's Guide series, she gives practical insight and suggestions laced with biblical teaching and sound advice. As the mother of four (2, 4, 27, and 28 year olds) and the grandmother of six, I found her series to be refreshing, encouraging, and applicable. This is a must-read series for new parents— encouraging, empowering, and equipping you in Christ to set your child up for success.

—Leslie Montgomery, Author of *A Parent's Guide to Spiritual Warfare*

When I was a young girl growing up in the 60s, my mother had a village! Upon bringing her baby home, her mama or mama-in-law, sister, or auntie had a suitcase planted next to the couch and faithfully stayed by the new mama's side for a week or more and helped with the baby. Once that loving family member packed up and left, neighbor mamas were readily available with expert advice and a casserole! With families now living further apart and more women working outside the home, today's mama isn't always so fortunate. Step in Erin MacPherson! Erin is that thoughtful friend, loving sister, and expert (whose resume includes changing 16,425 dirty diapers) who can ease mama's stress and hold her shaky hand through her first year as a mama. Not only should this book be on every new mama's nightstand, veteran mamas will also find some refreshing and new tricks of the trade!

—Debi Gutierrez, the "Mommy Comic" and Award-winning Actress, Talk Show Host, and Comedian

Erin MacPherson has written a parenting book that is engaging, delightful and humorous and most importantly, offers excellent insight in helping parents enrich their children spiritually in a very easy, relatable way.

—Jordyn Redwood, Pediatric ER Nurse
and Author of *Proof* and *Poison*

Erin MacPherson has a way of giving good, sound advice in the same way a mother might sneak a healthy dose of vitamins into a spoonful of ice cream. I chuckled my way through her pages until, by the end, I realized I'd received life-saving wisdom from above, through a friend walking alongside me.

—Faith Bogdan, Author of *Who Are All These Children and Why Are They Calling Me Mom?*

If you've recently been inducted into motherhood (or are preparing to do so in just a few shorts months), then let me just say, that this is the book for you. Jam-packed with information, insight, humor, and helpful advice that every new mommy will appreciate, this is the one guide that every Christian mama needs on her baby registry (not to mention her nightstand, too). Throughout *The Christian Mama's Guide to Baby's First Year*, Erin MacPherson provides her readers with the "ins and outs" as well as the "highs and lows" of practically every issue that new mommies must face when caring for their infants. Whether it's dealing with breast-feeding, a nocturnal newborn, or even post-partum depression, MacPherson's relatable style of writing and faith-driven message ensures that her readers have a friend (and a knowledgeable one at that) guiding them throughout their trials as first-time mothers. If you're going to be a mommy, or know someone who is, then there's plenty of information/advice to be gleaned by investing in this fabulous read.

—Jenny Sulpizio, Author of *Confessions of a Wonder Woman Wannabe*

THE
CHRISTIAN
MAMA'S
GUIDE
TO BABY'S FIRST YEAR

THE
CHRISTIAN MAMA'S GUIDE
TO BABY'S FIRST YEAR

———

Everything You

Need to Know to

Survive (*and Love*)

Your First Year as a Mom

———

BY ERIN MACPHERSON

THOMAS NELSON
Since 1798

NASHVILLE   DALLAS   MEXICO CITY   RIO DE JANEIRO

Published in Nashville, Tennessee, by Thomas Nelson. Thomas Nelson is a registered trademark of Thomas Nelson, Inc.

Author is represented by Books & Such Literary Agency.

Thomas Nelson, Inc., titles may be purchased in bulk for educational, business, fundraising, or sales promotional use. For information, please e-mail SpecialMarkets@ ThomasNelson.com.

Scripture quotations are taken from the Holy Bible, New International Version®, NIV®. Copyright © 1973, 1978, 1984, 2011 by Biblica, Inc.™ Used by permission of Zondervan. All rights reserved worldwide. www.zondervan.com

Library of Congress Control Number: 2013930849

ISBN: 9780849964749

Printed in the United States of America

13 14 15 16 17 RRD 5 4 3 2 1

To my babies:
My brave, strong, and hilarious Joey
My tender, generous, and witty Kate
and
My adventurous and exuberant Will.
You are my most precious gifts.

Contents

Acknowledgments

oli Deo Gloria. To God alone be the glory. That's my prayer for this book. I am acutely aware of the fact that every good gift comes from the Lord, and I am eternally grateful for everything He has given me—I am so blessed.

To my biggest blessings—my three precious children Joey, Kate, and Will—thank you for being the inspiration for so much of the content of this book and for making my journey as a mom worth walking. I love you each so much.

There is nothing I can say that can begin to show my gratitude to my incredibly supportive family: To my sister Alisa and my dad, who both meticulously line-edited every chapter of this book, giving me much-needed and much-appreciated advice, suggestions, and ideas. To my husband, Cameron, and my mom, who both watched my kids for countless hours so I could hole up in my office and write. And to my brother Troy, who brilliantly wrote down every daddy story he could think of in order to give me fodder for "The Christian Daddy's Guide to Babies" and "The Help-Daddy-Bond Initiative." I now tease him that he could ghostwrite for me. And he could.

Also, thanks to the generous, kind, compassionate, and faithful women with whom I have shared my baby-raising journey. Much love and gratitude to Anna Martin, Barbara Jones, Jessica Miller, Laura Marion-Faul, Michelle Halvorsen, Monica Scantlon, Rebecca Palmer, Rachel Spies, Sarah Jordan, Shellie Deringer, and Stevi Schuknecht. And to Brandi Alexander, Katie Scott, Kathi Lipp, Lucille Zimmerman, Hildi Nicksic, Derek Miller, Amanda Dykes, Mandy Fritsche, Sharmon Coleman, Donnine Souhrada,

Stacy Webster, and Janna Vaughn: thanks for stepping in one way or another to share your stories, your prayers, your support, and your editing expertise as I wrote this book.

I also need to give a big thank-you to the many medical professionals who shared insights, answered questions, and in other ways helped me make sure that the medical advice in this book was accurate. Special thanks to Jordyn Redwood, Soumya Adhikari, Esen Zentner, Amanda Ying, Bobbie Boyd, and Jeremy Gabrysh.

Finally, thank you to Rachelle Gardner, my agent from Books & Such Literary, who spent countless hours making sure this project actually happened. And to Debbie Wickwire, Adria Haley, and the team at Thomas Nelson, who have been incredibly insightful and meticulous in helping to make this book the best it can be.

Introduction

Welcome to Club Mom

Congratulations. You (yes, *you*) are an official, card-carrying member of the greatest club of all: Club Mom. And talk about an initiation ritual. You just survived months of morning sickness, forty (plus) pounds of weight gain, and seventeen hours of labor and delivery. Or, if you adopted, you trekked through seventy billion pages of paperwork, months of ups and downs, and nail-biting nerves. But you did it—and you did it all for that teeny, tiny, eight-ish-pound baby that you already love more than anything in the world.

I was inducted into the club two days after Christmas in 2005 when my son, Joey, was born. And what a day that was! I was exhausted. And groggy. And in pain. But I was overjoyed. My son was literally the most amazing, gorgeous, beautiful baby who had ever been born. (Yours is, too, right?) And from that moment on, I knew that Club Mom was exactly the place I wanted to be.

Isn't motherhood wonderful? I certainly don't need to tell you how fabulous your new baby is—but just for fun, let's talk about your baby for a minute. That downy-soft hair. Big, need-you eyes. Chubby round cheeks. Big ole potbelly. Fat, delicious knees. Tiny, stubby toes. Amazing! And adorable! And best of all, knit together by the Creator of the universe Himself with a very specific and wonderful purpose in mind. No wonder you feel so awestruck every time you sneak into your baby's nursery for one last good-night kiss.

Of course, just because you've been initiated into Club Mom doesn't mean you know what you're doing. I learned the hard way (read: through countless messy diaper blowouts) that motherhood has a huge learning curve. And nobody becomes a pro-mom—you know, the kind who carries a fully stocked diaper bag and manages to nurse her baby to sleep while picking up groceries—without practice . . . and some good, solid, mama-to-mama advice.

That's why I'm here—to get you from the spit-up–covered, baggy-eyed mama you are now, to the proud, camera-wielding, frosting-covered mama that you will be on your baby's first birthday. And what a journey it will be—in the next year, you'll learn how to sleep while simultaneously spoon-feeding your baby tiny pieces of cheese and recording your baby's adorable lip smacking; how to remove yellow stains from expensive, grandma-purchased, white baby clothes; and how to puree food using nothing but a spoon and your own ingenuity.

Yes, in the next year, you're going to learn a lot. How to care for your baby. How to be a godly mother. And how to embrace the ups and downs of motherhood while maintaining some semblance of the hip person you really are. As you can imagine, that's not an easy thing to do—especially when you're running on about three (interrupted) hours of sleep a night.

But, it is doable! And you're going to do great! So welcome to the club.

*A note for my particularly scrupulous readers: you may notice that most of the pronouns in this book are male. This was a decision made by my editors and me in order to keep the copy simple and consistent. It in no way means that this book is more applicable to boys or that I intended the tips and advice in this book to be just for boys. So, if you happen to have a daughter (like I do), please mentally substitute "her" for "him" and "she" for "he" as you read. And then write a very serious letter to whoever invented the English language letting them know how much easier our lives would be if pronouns weren't gender specific.

ONE

Getting into the New Mama Groove

Surviving and Thriving as a New Mom

Being a new mom isn't as easy as it looks. I remember going to the grocery store when my son was a few months old and standing in line behind a woman who had three kids. She stood there, thumbing through a magazine, with her baby sleeping peacefully in a sling while her two older (and perfectly behaved) children sat quietly in the cart and quizzed each other on phonics. *Phonics.* No joke! And to top it all off, the woman was wearing real pants (not sweats), and I think I spotted a smidgen of mascara on her eyelashes. My jaw dropped in awe. How did she *do* that?

Meanwhile I stood there wearing a ratty, spit-up–covered T-shirt, my hair in a greasy ponytail, bouncing up and down in line while singing "Jesus Loves Me," to try to make my son stop screaming so I could at least make it through the checkout line and buy milk. And I wondered how I was ever going to be able to do normal things—like go to the grocery store or (gasp!) have a social life—without enduring a total meltdown (both the baby's and mine).

Being a mom is hard. Way back in the 1960s, two psychologists named Holmes and Rah decided to study the link between major life events and stress. They did a bunch of research and interviewed a ton of people and came to the startling conclusion that major life changes—you know, like having a baby—are *stressful*. Um, well, duh.

Of course having a new baby is stressful! In a matter of minutes, you go from a fashionable, intelligent, and totally (okay, mostly) put-together woman to a blubbering, still-trying-to-lose-the-baby-weight mother who is exhausted, overwhelmed, and trying to figure out how to use the nasal aspirator. It's a huge life change—and most mamas (like me!) need some time to get the hang of it.

But you'll get there. Okay, so chances are you'll probably never stand in line at the grocery store while your kid discusses the intricacies of phonics, but you'll certainly get to the point where you can manage to put on real pants and buy milk without feeling like a bumbling fool. I promise.

How to Get into the New Mom Groove

1. Give yourself a break.

Remember that seemingly perfect mom I told you about earlier in the chapter? The one who managed to wear pants *and* mascara while wrangling three kids? Well, fabulous as she is, you have to remember that she has three kids . . . which means she's had a lot of practice. I'm willing to bet that there was a point in time when she also stood in the grocery store with a screaming baby in her arms while covered in spit-up from head to toe.

You're not going to have the mom thing down pat right away—or ever. Case in point: We flew from Texas to Oregon right around my son's first birthday. With a full year's experience of being a mom under my belt, I had everything under control. Or so I thought. Right after we got on the plane, I realized that my son had a dirty diaper—and of course, in the process of trying to change it on the cramped plane, I managed to completely soil his pants, his shirt, *and* his sweater. I reached for the diaper bag—only to realize that I had checked it. I had nothing. Well, nothing except for a naked baby on an airplane in December.

Every mom has a story like that—well, maybe not exactly like that, but I'm pretty sure every mom forgets to bring a change of clothes once or twice. And when things happen that make us look inexperienced or clueless or just plain frazzled, we have to take it in stride. Realize we're doing the best we can. And confidently ask everyone around us if we can please borrow a diaper.

2. Give yourself a break from baby.

You heard me. If you're going to stay sane, you need to pry yourself away from your little schnookums every once in a while. I'm not telling you to go away on a four-week African safari, but it certainly wouldn't hurt you to sneak out of the room while your baby is sleeping and take a shower. Or if you're feeling really brave, you could leave your baby with your mom and go out to the Tastee Freez with your husband.

The point is that as wonderful as your baby is, you need some time to be *you*. And seeing as how you weren't always a brand-new mom with a brand-new baby attached to your hip, it's good for you to pry that baby off your hip every once in a while and go back to being your fabulous self—give or take ten to fifteen pounds.

When my son was a few weeks old, my husband suggested (okay, demanded) that I leave the baby with him and go to the mall with my sister. I whined and moaned and worried that something would happen. But I eventually left. And we had a great time. We were only gone an hour or two (I was breast-feeding), but I remember feeling so liberated walking around carrying just my purse. I felt like a real person again!

3. Pace yourself.

When you have a new baby in tow, there is no way you can do all the things you used to do back in the day. That's fine. It's okay that the house only gets vacuumed when your mother-in-law comes or that an entire day's worth of activities constitutes a run to Target to buy diapers. Yes, you headed up the world committee on organic gardening while holding down a full-time job and a seventy-hour-per-week volunteer ministry in your pre-baby days, but you just aren't going to be able to do that now that you have kids. And that's okay.

The good news is that you'll get back into your do-everything-and-volunteer-at-the-soup-kitchen-to-boot groove soon enough. I remember feeling so incompetent when my son was a newborn. I felt as if nothing got accomplished at my house. Ever. But you know what? My son didn't stay a newborn and I didn't stay a newborn mom forever. Now I head the snack committee for my son's football league and organize the class picnic and write the newsletter for my MOPS group. And some days, I kind of miss those nostalgic new-mom days when my only daily responsibility was making sure my son got fed.

4. Let your friends help.

It takes a whole village—or at least an entire extended family and a church group—to raise a child. And yet so many young mamas try to do it alone. I remember being nervous when my friends offered to set up a CareCalendar (www.carecalendar.org) to bring me meals after my baby was born. I didn't want them to think I wasn't capable—and I certainly didn't want them to feel that they had to wait on me. Of course, they didn't feel that way at all. They wanted to help—just as I do when my friends have babies.

Here's the way I look at it: when you have a brand-new baby and are recovering from what was possibly a very traumatic labor, you need all the help you can get. So accept whatever your friends and family offer you gratefully—and make a mental note to do the same when they need you. And the truth is, unless you're still asking your friends to make you dinner and clean your house when your baby is ten months old, no one will feel as though they're waiting on you. They love you. They want to bless you. And you'd do the same for them in a heartbeat.

5. Try to maintain a sense of normalcy.

Yes, your house is messy. No, your clothes don't fit. Yes, you feel like a completely different person than you were before your baby was born. But that doesn't mean everything has to change. Try to do one thing every day that the "old" you would've done—whether it's obsessively de-cluttering the kitchen counter or simply putting on a coat of mascara.

When my son was a new baby, I made myself a little "get yourself together" schedule. Okay, I didn't call it that, but every day I "scheduled" one household task or errand or job to do so that I felt as though I had responsibilities outside of slouching on the couch, with my boob in my son's mouth, while watching TLC. Some of my jobs were easy—like reading the new issue of *Parenting* from cover to cover. Others were a bit more difficult, like trying to figure out how to make the wipe-warmer actually keep wipes warm.

. . . .

Time-Out for Mom

For When You're Just Getting into the
Swing of the New Mom Thing

"He tends his flock like a shepherd: He gathers the lambs in his arms and carries them close to his heart; he gently leads those that have young." (Isaiah 40:11)

Father God, what a blessing my new baby is. There is nothing You could've given me that is more wonderful, more beautiful, and more telling of Your love. Thank You. And Lord, while my life has totally changed, thank You for dealing gently with me and showering me with Your grace when I need it most. Lead me, Lord God, so that I can raise this precious baby in a way that guides him to Your kingdom. Amen.

. . . .

Ways You've Changed Since Becoming a Mom

- **The old you**: Wore cute, belly-hugging tops and styled your hair every single day without fail.
- **The new you**: Has been wearing the same pajamas now for a week. (In your defense, they're really, really cute pajamas.)
- **The old you**: Never missed an episode of *Downton Abbey*.
- **The new you**: Never misses an episode of the *Late, Late Show*. Ever. (What else are you supposed to do when lil' Mr. Hungrypants is always wanting to eat at 1 a.m.?)
- **The old you**: Knew how to make a mean grilled-cheese sandwich.
- **The new you**: Has grilled-cheese sandwiches for dinner. Three times every week.
- **The old you**: Skipped out on the super-long and boring HOA meeting because it was super-long and boring.
- **The new you**: Wishes you could go to the super-long and boring HOA meeting (at least it'd get you out of the house) but can't because it's during your baby's nap time.
- **The old you**: Never had time to lunch with your girlfriends.
- **The new you**: Lets your baby nap in the infant seat while you have lunch with your girlfriends, whom you haven't seen for weeks.
- **The old you**: Felt guilty if you went to bed without doing the dinner dishes.

~⌒ **The new you**: Spends the entire day watching your sweet baby sleep—and is completely okay with the fact that the same cereal bowl has been sitting in the sink for a week.

Christian Mama Style

True story: When I told my friend that I was writing a Christian pregnancy guide, she said, "Every pregnant mom experiences the same morning sickness and the same weight gain. So why would I need a special pregnancy guide just for Christian moms? Seems like any old pregnancy guide would say the exact same things."

And she's right—sort of. Yes, every mom, Christian or not, shares similar experiences as she learns to navigate being a parent. Every mom feels that intense I-will-never-be-able-to-get-over-how-amazing-you-are feeling while simultaneously freaking out about the fact that she is entirely and utterly responsible for the tiny life in her arms. We mama bears are fiercely protective of our babies—both physically and emotionally—and we'll do anything and everything we can to make sure our babies are safe, healthy, and happy. It's human nature.

But what makes Christian moms different is that we also care deeply about our families' relationships with Jesus along the way. We want to grow closer to Jesus in this journey of parenthood, and we want our kids to grow up to love Him with all of their hearts, souls, and minds. And in the meantime we also want to teach our kids character, help them grow rock-solid faiths, sow in them a joyful hope in Jesus, and help them to realize that while they are flawed human beings, they serve a God who is perfect yet forgiving and loving yet powerful. A tall order. But, before you really start to freak out (I know the very thought of that makes my mind start to whir with thoughts of my own unworthiness), I want to remind you that it is God who can and will work in your kids' lives. It is God who knit them together with a perfect plan in mind for their lives. And it is God who will work to help that plan come into fruition. Isn't that a relief?

Of course, we as parents aren't totally off the hook. God calls us to love and nurture our children in the fear and admonition of the Lord. And that starts from day one. Yes, that's right. You can start teaching your baby about Jesus from the day he or she is born. Here are a few easy ways to do just that.

1. **Pray**. It's probably a given that most Christian moms pray for their kids. But I also know what it's like to be in that crazy newborn phase where there's never enough time for basics like sleeping or showering. And when I was in that phase, prayer time often got relegated to the back burner. I want to encourage you to get in the habit of praying for your kids— and praying often. One way I've found to be purposeful about prayer is to use Scripture to pray for your kids. (The book *Praying God's Word for Your Life* by Kathi Lipp has some great ideas on how to do this.) I've spent the last six months reading the book of Ephesians and then using the words in that portion of scripture to pray for my three kids. It's been a powerful experience where God has revealed a lot to me about His plan for them.

2. **Adjust your expectations**. One thing I had to learn as a new mom was that my time with Jesus was just different than before I had kids. In my pre-kid days, I would often set aside extended periods of time every morning to pray and read my Bible. If I needed more time with God, I could just set my alarm a little earlier. But I think any mom will tell you that a baby is no match for an alarm clock and that it's almost a guarantee that if you set an alarm for 6:00 a.m., your baby will wake up at ten to six. Because of this, I had to learn to take mini prayer breaks throughout the day as well as find alternative times (like during my baby's nap) to read my Bible.

3. **Sing songs**. I love the song "Change My Heart, O God," so when my daughter was tiny, I would sit in my rocker, snuggle

her against me, and sing that song over and over. For months and months, that's how she fell asleep. And even now, more than four years later, she still sings that song, loudly and clearly, whenever she's down or upset. It has become a comfort to her.

4. **Set an example**. Get into the habit of spending thirty minutes each morning—at a time when your baby can see you and hear you—reading your Bible and praying. Sure, a two-month-old isn't going to know what's going on, but as your baby grows and recognizes that Mommy spends time every day in the same spot, praying to God, he or she may be inspired to do the same.

5. **Expose them to the Bible**. I get that busting out a King James Version with a six-month-old will probably only fly for fourteen seconds, but try giving your kids access to the Bible in age-appropriate chunks. Point out a rainbow in the sky and talk about the story of Noah's ark. Read short Bible stories from a children's Bible. Talk about how God created everything we see in the world. As your baby grows, these simple conversations will be woven in with experiences to become part of his spiritual legacy.

Being a Mom Rocks!

The truth is that being a mom is the best thing ever—regardless of how many diapers you've changed or how many times your baby woke you up last night. Your baby is pretty much the most amazing thing that has happened to you. And aside from the fact that your life is a teensy bit nuttier than it's ever been before, your life is also so much sweeter. Nothing beats baby smiles, melodic gurgles, and chubby baby knees. Nothing.

Plus, when you have a new baby, you feel as if you're a rock star. Everywhere you go, people will point and ooh and ahh and try to get a glimpse underneath the baby blanket. People will hold doors open for your baby stroller and give you advice on elevators. People will strike up conversations with you, wistfully thinking about the days when their now–thirty-year-olds were that small. And everyone—and I mean everyone—will marvel at how strong/smart/alert/quiet/sweet your baby is.

Even when things start to feel tough—like when your baby wakes you up seventeen times in the middle of the night and you've gone through an entire package of diapers in twenty-four hours—there's nothing that will ever damper the feeling you have for that baby in your arms. Nothing. In my new mom days, I was completely in awe of my son and the love I felt for him.

Experiencing that kind of love showed me a lot about the love God has for us. Of course, we could never love like He does, but just the experience of being a mom and loving a child made me overwhelmingly grateful. In 1 John 3:1, the Bible tell us to "see what great love the Father has lavished on us, that we should be called children of God! And that is what we are!" God loves me more than I could ever comprehend—yet holding my son for the first time, I got a glimpse of it. What an amazing feeling.

Anyway, now that you have your mama groove, it's time to talk about the nitty-gritty of newborn parenting. How do you change your baby's diaper without getting pee all over yourself? How do you know when his cries are real or when he's just working out a secret plan to keep you awake all night long? And how in the world do you get those crazy (but adorable) button-up jumpsuits buttoned when your baby is squirming and wiggling? Let's find out.

TWO

The Christian Mama's Lying-In Period

Postpartum Healing, Emotions, Hormones, and More

Whether your baby just slipped out in one push that you hardly even noticed or you pushed for thirteen hours and ended up having a C-section, I'm going to go ahead and say that your birthing experience was traumatic. And while I totally believe that God created us for this purpose and equipped us with everything we need to thrive and survive as childbearing mamas, that doesn't mean that childbirth isn't the most ridiculously traumatizing thing a woman can go through. And there aren't enough butt-sized bags of ice in the world to make me think otherwise.

But you did it! And you have a beautiful baby in your arms right now to remind you that every *hoo-hoo-hee* and "Let's just throw a couple more stitches in there just to make sure" was worth it. Because your baby is out. And if that's not enough to make you positively giddy, the fact that your baby is out means you're not pregnant anymore. And that's cause for celebration. No more weight gain. No more stretch marks. No more middle-of-the-night corn dog cravings. No more pregnancy insomnia. (We don't have to mention new baby insomnia just yet.) Just that sweet, doe-eyed little wonder staring up at you.

Of course, all that trauma means you have some recovering to do. A few months ago, I downloaded the book called *The Prospective Mother: A Handbook for Women During Pregnancy,* written by an MD at Johns Hopkins back in 1912. The book is full of fascinating tidbits that make me grateful to be a mother in the twenty-first century, instead of in 1912. Perhaps the most interesting thing to me was the fact that doctors believed back then that women shouldn't even stand up for six weeks (yes, that's *weeks*) after childbirth. They called it the lying-in period, and a typical family would hire a nurse to come live with them for two months after a child was born so the mom could spend her days completely uninterrupted and relaxed.

I'm going to go ahead and guess that six weeks of lying-in just isn't practical for you and your family—can you even imagine how much it would cost to hire a real, trained nurse to live with you for two months?—but I think we can learn from this. Because even as your pain dissipates and your body starts to heal, you did go through a lot of trauma, and reminding yourself to take it easy for a few weeks can only help you recover more quickly.

So I'm making it official: I'm implementing a Christian Mama Lying-in Period for all new moms. And as part of that lying-in period, I'm going to boss you around a little and make you do a few things to make sure you recover as quickly as possible. There's even a contract to be signed by you, your husband, and the person most likely to bring you non-fat decaf lattes in bed when you need them most. Read it carefully, sign it, and then stick to it. I promise: you'll thank me in six weeks.

Official Contract for
The Christian Mama Lying-In Period

I, _____, am officially declaring the six weeks following the birth of my baby a lying-in period, Christian Mama Style. During this lying-in period, I solemnly promise to:

- Relax. I won't feel guilty when I spend the entire afternoon watching *Law & Order* reruns and then "cook" Rice Krispies for dinner.
- Focus on taking care of myself and my baby without worrying about things like unpacking my hospital bag, taking down the Christmas lights, or vacuuming the floor. (Unless, of course, the white noise from the vacuum helps the baby sleep, then I'll do it as often as necessary.)
- Let my baby fall asleep on my lap and then use that time when I'm forced to sit to pray, read, or do something else relaxing. I will save tasks like writing to-do lists, developing a business plan for the company I dreamed up during last night's midnight feeding session, or inventing a breast pump that works while I'm sleeping for after my lying-in period.
- Sleep when my baby sleeps. Even if there are four-day old dirty dishes in the sink and piles of laundry in the living room, my sleep will take priority.
- Let people help me. I won't feel guilty when my best friend brings me a tray of lasagna or my mother-in-law offers to fold all of those piles of laundry. Because they love me. And I would do the same for them in a heartbeat.
- Treasure this time. Yes, I'm exhausted and overwhelmed (and flabby) but my baby will only be tiny once. And I will treasure every feeding session, every coo, and every smile that's probably just gas but still looks awfully cute.

Signed: _____

Husband: _____

Witness: _____

Healing *Down There*

My sister, Alisa, told me that after she had her daughter, just thinking about what had happened *down there* made her shudder. And the mere thought of going pee or—worse—eventually having sex made her want to start crying. And since the mere thought of the trauma your lady parts have sustained probably makes you want to cover your ears and start humming "I Will Survive," I'm sure this section won't be easy for you to read. But I'm going to give it to you straight—no holding back—because I can pretty much guarantee that what you're imagining is worse than reality. Or at least just as bad as reality.

Let's just start with the basics. Look at your baby. Look at her head. That cute little head—the one with that sweet baby hair and those tiny rosebud lips—just squeezed out through your vagina. And, even though your vagina probably did a fantastic job of stretching to help that happen, chances are you still suffered some sort of vaginal tearing in childbirth. Some doctors and midwives will snip your vagina on purpose—called an episiotomy—to help the baby come out, but most will just let you tear naturally, as they've found that women who tear naturally heal quicker.

Regardless, your doctor or midwife may have rattled off some numbers and letters to go with your tearing, saying something like, "Wow, you have stage 4 tearing on that left sidewall" or, "Just a little stage 2 anterior tear." And while these numbers and stages do a lot for future bragging rights, the truth is that all vaginal tearing hurts. And no matter the stage, tearing isn't a fun thing to deal with.

The first thing the doctor or midwife will do after your baby is born and your placenta is expelled is look around down there to check out the damage. At this point, you'll probably have your baby in your arms, so you'll be pretty distracted (a good thing), and so you probably won't feel much. Once the damage has been assessed, you'll probably need some stitches. Fortunately, if you're still numb from your epidural, you won't feel this at all, and even if you gave birth naturally, your vaginal area will be so numb from childbirth that the stitches will feel like mere pinpricks.

Once you're all stitched up and your lady parts are realigned, they'll pop a bag of ice under your bum and let you try to forget about what just happened and focus on what really matters: your baby. Over the next few days, your nurses will probably check you down there from time to time and make sure you have a fresh ice bag every hour or so to bring down the swelling, but overall, you can remain mostly oblivious to the state of your health down there while you're in the hospital. But there will be a point (for instance when your husband hits a speed bump while he's driving you home from the hospital) when you'll realize how much you really hurt down there. And just as you reach the realization that you're really hurting, you'll also realize that you're on your own for taking care of it. Here's how to help yourself heal.

Tips to Help Yourself Heal Down There

1. **Follow your doctor's, nurse's, or midwife's instructions implicitly.** It may seem a bit strange to squirt yourself with warm water from a squirt bottle every time you use the restroom for a few weeks, but I'm pretty sure we can all agree that getting an infection down there doesn't sound fun.
2. **Don't be afraid to take your painkillers.** My sister-in-law, Annie, had such severe tearing after she gave birth to my nephew that her doctor prescribed Vicodin. He eased her fears of taking a high-powered pain reliever by explaining that when her body wasn't focused on the pain, it could heal more quickly. So you can probably assume that if your doctor prescribes painkillers, you probably have enough damage to warrant their use.
3. **Don't forget your stool softeners.** Your doctor or midwife

will undoubtedly prescribe some sort of stool softener for you to take for the first few weeks after you have your baby. I don't want to get too explicit here, but basically, if your stool is softer, it'll be easier to push out and less traumatizing on your traumatized parts. Just don't forget to drink lots of water, too, to help this process along.

4. **Change your sanitary pads regularly**. You're going to be bleeding down there for a few weeks (see "Lochia"), and keeping yourself clean down there is yet another simple way to prevent infection and help your body heal more quickly.

5. **Rest as much as possible**. I think it goes without saying that if you're doing jumping jacks and other calisthenics while you recover, the healing will probably take longer.

The First Trip to the Toilet

I wish I could say that you could just plug your ears and say, "La la la!" and try to ignore what's going on down there. But unfortunately, you can't. Because there's one thing you'll have to do that will remind you fairly quickly and shockingly exactly what type of trauma you've experienced. I'm sure you can guess what that one thing is.

I had C-sections, so I've never dealt with this, but my friends who delivered their babies vaginally have all emphatically said that while that first trip to the bathroom is terrifying, it's not as bad as you'd expect it to be. My friend Angie told me that she lay in bed for six hours—that's right, 360 minutes—just getting up the nerve to go to the bathroom. She finally had to pee so bad that she just couldn't hold it, and even then sat on the toilet, clenching for twenty minutes—just overcoming her fear of letting a trickle get out. She said it hurt. But not as bad as she had expected.

Five Things You May Need to Know About Post-Childbirth Potty Breaks

1. **It may be hard to get started**. If you had an epidural or a C-section, you probably had a catheter. This, along with the trauma of childbirth, can really irritate your bladder. Which means you may sit on the toilet, trying to pee, for twenty minutes before you're able to squeeze even a tiny bit of pee out. Likewise, once you start peeing, your urine stream may stop even before your bladder is fully empty. Take your time. This is normal.

2. **It will be bloody**. I'm not sure there is much that can prepare you for the amount of blood you'll lose immediately after childbirth—but let me just tell you that your first trip to the bathroom will be bloody. Like I-think-something-may-have-burst-in-there bloody. But most of the time, postpartum bleeding—even significant postpartum bleeding—is entirely normal. Just to be safe, your nurse or midwife will probably ask you to pee/bleed into a cup to check your urine output as well as blood loss.

3. **Keep your toilet supplies handy**. You're going to need a lot of gear to go to the bathroom for the first couple of days. My nurse at the hospital put together a cute little toilet basket fully stocked with maxi pads, those horrible netted underwear you get in the hospital, a spray bottle, and some wet wipes and put it on the counter in the bathroom. That way I had all the supplies I needed at arm's reach.

4. **You may need some help getting up and down**. Yes, this may make you feel decrepit and old, but when you consider the fact that you just went through not only the trauma of childbirth but also nine months of pregnancy that stretched your abdominal muscles to the max, it's just fine to need a little help getting on and off the toilet for a few days.

5. **Don't wear nice clothes into the bathroom.** Right after I had Will, I changed into some new, cute PJ pants right before I headed to the bathroom, thinking I was going to get fresh and clean and ready for visitors. Thirty minutes later, said PJ pants were crumpled on the floor and covered in a disgusting mix of water and blood, and I couldn't even bend down to pick them up. I'm sure that's way too much information—remember I told you I was going to give it to you straight—but your best bet is to wear a ratty old hospital gown for your first few trips to the loo.

C-section Healing

I had three C-sections, so I never really had to deal with all the hoo-ha healing issues that moms who have vaginal births do. But trust me: a C-section definitely doesn't let you off the hook. Because what you avoided in trauma to your nether regions, you made up for with trauma to your entire abdominal wall. Which isn't exactly an easy thing to heal from.

Three hours after my nephew Jacob was delivered (vaginally), I went to visit and found my sister-in-law Annie sitting up in bed, eating a bagel. I stood there aghast, remembering the entire day I spent in a post C-section haze and the two entire days I had to go without food after my first C-section. (Apparently there is a rule that women have to pass gas before they get on the food-delivery rotation.) I was eight months pregnant with my second at the time, and as soon as I left the hospital room, I called my doctor and asked if there was any way I could try a vaginal birth after C-section. Now, I'm not calling a vaginal birth easy—I know it's anything but—but being recovered enough to eat a bagel within two hours of giving birth was enough incentive for me to try.

I ended up having a C-section again—my doctor didn't think a vaginal birth attempt was safe since my first two pregnancies were so close together—but I'm still slightly jealous of how quickly my

The Christian Mama's Guide to Baby's First Year

friends who have had vaginal births were able to recover both physically and mentally. That said, each time I spent three days in the hospital recovering, and within two weeks, I could get up and down out of a chair without much pain. Here's how to help your healing after a C-section.

Tips to Help You Heal after a C-section

1. **Take your meds.** With my first, I had the brilliant idea to just skip the trip to the pharmacy on our way home from the hospital and try to go pain-med free. I have no idea why I thought this was a good idea—can you say postpartum hormones?—but let's just say that my husband went on a fun little excursion to the pharmacy about three hours later. My advice: take your pain meds as prescribed for the first week and after that if you want to slowly wean yourself off of them, call your doctor to come up with a plan.

2. **Call your doctor if you have shoulder or back pain.** Here's some fancy medical knowledge that you may not know: the nerves that run into your diaphragm are connected to the nerves in your shoulders and upper back. I learned this completely useless fact after my third C-section when I started having excruciating shoulder pain. I was in so much pain that my husband called my doctor, who explained to me that postpartum shoulder and back pain is often the result of damage or bruising to the diaphragm during a C-section. This isn't dangerous—and can often be eased by taking a short walk, getting a massage, or taking an anti-inflammatory—but if you're feeling intense shoulder pain, let your doctor know so he or she can help you feel better.

3. **Get up and move.** Now, I'm not asking you to pop in a Jazzercise DVD and don your leg warmers, but a short jaunt around the maternity ward or your house can really help

speed up the healing. So, whenever you're up for it, make it your goal to go on a five-minute walk every hour.

4. **Keep everything you need within arm's reach**. I know I just told you to get up and move, but let me just tell you that actually getting up to go move can be really painful. So limit your up-and-down trips to pure emergencies (e.g., midnight snacks) and avoid getting up for unnecessary reasons (e.g., to grab the remote control). My suggestion is to have your husband put everything you could possibly need in the next hour—a book, the remote, your cell phone, your laptop—right next to you so you can settle in and rest.

5. **Drink lots of water**. I'm not sure if this is medically proven, but the old wives say that your body is able to heal more quickly if it's hydrated. And since water is also essential to establish breast-feeding, drinking lots of water is a no-brainer.

Lochia

Warning: If you're not a mom, but instead, say, you picked up this book and started reading when you saw it on the coffee table at your friend's house, I highly recommend that you skip this section. This is one of those things that may just scare you away from wanting to have a baby. Ever. (And if you've already gotten this far in the book without getting freaked out, then this could just push you over the edge.) So, new and expecting moms, read on. The rest of you, skip ahead to page 110 where you'll learn all about the totally impractical yet adorable baby items you can buy for your sweet friend who let you borrow this book.

Now, for the rest of you. You know how everyone has been telling you for nine months that the upside to being pregnant is that you don't have your period for nine months? As if missing your period nine times totally makes up for all the morning sickness, weight gain, and back pain you've experienced. What these well-meaning folks haven't told you is that once you have your baby, your body will make up for all those missed periods by releasing all of the stuff it's been holding on to in order to nourish and protect your baby.

And not to be graphic, but it's going to be bloody. For three to six weeks, if medical websites are to be believed. And during those three to six weeks, you'll have to not only work really hard to keep that area clean (see "Tips to Help Yourself Heal Down There") but also to be somewhat observant of said discharge so you can report anything unusual to your doctor or midwife. If you need a cheat sheet on what "unusual" means, you can pretty much assume that as long as you're not passing clots bigger than a plum and the discharge doesn't smell bad, you're probably fine. If you notice huge, huge clots and a nasty smell, hop on the phone with your medical provider right away, because you may have an infection.

The Hormone Flood

A few hours after my son Will was born, my husband fell asleep on the couch in my hospital room with his shoes on. Now, given that we had been up half of the night dealing with contractions before a 4:30 a.m. hospital check-in for my C-section, you may think that him falling asleep was a perfectly acceptable thing to do. You may even think that he was probably exhausted, and since both the baby and I were sound asleep, it was a good time for him to grab a catnap as well. But you would be thinking wrong.

Because clearly—at least clearly in a hormone-fueled, postpartum mom's brain—any man who falls asleep with his shoes on in a hospital room is trying to send a message to his wife that he is mad at her for making him stay up all night and sleep in an uncomfortable bed, to boot. And since he's so mad, he probably wants her to wake him up from his much-needed catnap to deal with a tear-fueled sobbing session about how she didn't mean to keep him up all night, and if she had been able to choose, she would've had the baby at five in the afternoon. Makes total sense, right?

I think any mom who has had a baby will tell you that one of the most shocking parts of the post-childbirth experience is the flood of hormones that hits you about an hour or two after your baby is born. For me, it resulted in intense mood swings that left me sobbing one minute, angry the next, and giddy with joy five minutes later. This is completely normal—although a bit agitating to exhausted daddies who just want to sleep a bit—and can be contributed to the bazillions of hormones that flood your body as your baby is born. That said, if you're having a hard time dealing with it, talk to your doctor, nurse, or midwife about how you feel. Medical professionals have all sorts of tricks on how you can get through it.

The Baby Blues

Part of the aforementioned hormone flood is a super-common condition called "the baby blues." The baby blues is minor depression or anxiety that shows up in as many as 75 percent of postpartum moms within the first few days of having a baby.

I remember arriving home after my daughter, Kate, was born to big signs that said "It's a Girl!" in my yard and fresh, hot, just-delivered pizza in the kitchen. My whole family had gathered to welcome us home—and while it was about the sweetest thing they could do, I completely melted down in tears. I was so overwhelmed with indescribable emotions that I literally couldn't have a conversation with anyone. Looking back, it was clearly the baby blues.

If you notice yourself crying at the drop of a hat in the days after your baby is born, don't panic that you've been transformed into a blubbery, emotional mess. Because most likely it's the baby blues, and it will go away within a few days once your hormones get balanced out.

Postpartum Depression

Before I move on, I want to make sure I address the fact that a slight case of the baby blues—something a lot of moms experience—is not to be confused with or mistaken for postpartum depression (PPD). PPD is a serious, hormone-caused illness that goes far beyond the typical exhaustion-fueled hormone-craze that all moms experience. It's very serious. Like call-your-doctor-right-now serious.

One of my best friends, Anna, had severe postpartum depression after she had her second baby. To give you a little background, Anna is a vibrant, smart, savvy, and fun Christian mom who never fails to be there for her friends, her kids, and her husband. She's amazing—the kind of girl who manages to juggle her career and her kids and her house and her life (and run marathons) with grace and ease.

So as you can imagine, when her husband, Bryan, found her hiding in her bedroom for hours, crying nonstop and completely unable to function, he knew that something very serious was wrong. It was as if she was a completely different person. When she started having suicidal thoughts—as well as talking as if her new baby, Alice, belonged to someone else—both Bryan and Anna knew she needed help.

Fortunately for Anna, her doctor took her condition very seriously. He stepped in right away and made sure she got the help she needed. And now, six months later, Anna is back to being her normal, fun-loving, manage-two-kids-and-a-career-and-a-golden-retriever-with-grace-and-poise self. But it was hard. And since she knows how hard it was, she met with me for lunch and gave me some ideas on how to help women who are suffering from PPD.

Helping Yourself When You Have PPD

⤳ **Call your doctor.** PPD is very serious, and your doctor has a whole repertoire of medications that can help. Anna wanted me to make sure to tell you that if you don't feel that the medication is helping, call your doctor again. It took her a few tries to find a medication that worked for her, but once they honed in on the right prescription, she started to feel much better.

- ∽ **Talk to a counselor**. My friend Lucille Zimmerman—a licensed counselor who also authored a book about how women can take care of themselves in the midst of difficult situations—told me that when a woman is suffering from PPD, she not only needs medicinal therapy, but she also needs help learning how to cope with the huge changes that have happened in her life. A qualified Christian counselor can help with that.
- ∽ **Be willing to accept help**. It's hard to accept help from others—especially when you're used to being the self-sufficient supermom that you are—but it's important. Not only will you get the help you need—trust me: the last thing you need to worry about right now is the laundry—but you'll also get much-needed time to rest and heal.
- ∽ **Get away**. PPD is not one of those fight-through-it illnesses. It's serious. And you may need some time to get away by yourself to heal. And I want to reassure you that it's totally fine—no, admirable—to be willing to leave your baby with grandma or a friend and take a day or two to heal.

Helping Your Wife or Friend Who Has PPD

When Anna and I were talking about PPD, she told me that her husband, Bryan, literally saved her life in the months that followed her pregnancy. And Anna isn't giving him all that credit for nothing. I can see how the way he responded really was the catalyst that started her healing. When Anna got sick, the first thing Bryan did was rally her entire support network to surround her and carry her through that difficult time. He stood behind her, making sure she got the help she needed, and selflessly stepped in and carried her load until she healed. Everyone all together now: *Awww*.

I think we all want to be Bryan for our friends and family members who are suffering. We all want to be the support structure our loved ones need and can depend on. But we don't always know how. Here are some of Bryan and Anna's suggestions on things you can do to help:

1. **Visit**. When Anna first got sick, Bryan called all of Anna's closest friends and asked us if we could visit her whenever possible. So we set up a calendar so that one person went to Anna's house to visit every single day. Anna says that there were days when she just wanted to hole up and ignore her ringing doorbell, but as she started to recover, she realized that she was looking forward to those visits. And it felt good to know that she had a huge support network standing behind her.

2. **Talk . . . and listen when she's ready**. Another close friend of mine, Rebecca, also suffered from PPD. When Anna got sick, Rebecca e-mailed and told Anna about her experiences with PPD and let her know that when she was ready to talk about how she was feeling, she would be there. Anna said she ignored the e-mail for a while, but after her medications started to kick in, she called Rebecca, and they had a long conversation about their struggles. It was great to have a listening ear—especially a listening ear that understood exactly what she was going through.

3. **Intervene**. Even if your friend or wife insists she's okay, it's your job to intervene when she needs help. That means doing anything and everything—even physically taking her to the hospital or removing her from a dangerous situation—to make sure she gets the help she needs.

4. **Pray**. Perhaps the most powerful thing you can do to help a friend is pray for her. And let her know you're praying by sending her an e-mail or text message to encourage her that

she is not struggling alone, but instead has the backing of the almighty God. How's that for reassurance?

· ·

Time-Out for Mom

For When You're Feeling Down, Anxious,
or Depressed as a New Mom

"Praise be to the God and Father of our Lord Jesus Christ, the Father of compassion and the God of all comfort, who comforts us in all our troubles, so that we can comfort those in any trouble with the comfort we ourselves receive from God." (2 Corinthians 1:3–4)

Jesus, You are the Lord of comfort and peace. And right now, I need you to wrap Your loving arms around me and fill me with Your Spirit. I am struggling right now, Lord, and I pray that You give me the strength I need to survive the days, the hours, and the minutes that I face. Lord, give me the ability to know my limits, to ask for help when I need it, and to rely on You wholeheartedly. Amen.

· ·

A Pain in the Breast

In my pre-kid days, my breasts weren't really a pressing concern in my life. Sure, I tried to buy bras that fit and made sure my nipples didn't show through my shirts, but overall, I rarely thought about my breasts. And when I did, it was a quick breast self-check, and then I went on with my day.

But then baby #1 was born, and by the end of his first week of life, my breasts had not only become the center of his world, but had jumped up to being quite the priority in my life as well. Why? Because they hurt. A lot. And since they hurt, feeding my baby as often as he seemed to want to eat was excruciating. Not to be dramatic or anything.

Now that I've made you all stressed, let me give you a big heaping dose of reassurance: yes, they hurt now, but they won't hurt forever. In fact, once you get through the initial I-want-to-scream-every-time-my-baby-gets-within-six-feet-of-my-body pain, breast-feeding is actually quite painless. It's called the "fourteen-day phenomenon"—you have to survive the first two weeks and let this formerly ignored part of your body get used to constant sucking and touching and filling and refilling—and then things will be much better. To learn more about that, flip ahead to the breast-feeding chapter on page 65. In the meantime, here's how to deal with the pain.

Sore Nipples

More likely than not, your nipples aren't used to the type (and sheer quantity) of friction that comes from a suckling baby. So, as your baby practices her latching and suckling skills, your nipples have to practice getting sucked on. And in most cases, the skin gets sore, raw, and cracked as it tries to adjust to all of that attention. I can go ahead and assure you that 90 percent of new moms will tell you that this is the most painful part of breast-feeding—and while excruciating, your nipples should heal fairly quickly. From that point on, they shouldn't hurt at all.

For years, the gold standard for nipple pain and cracking has been a cream called Lansinoh. It's pretty expensive—like twelve dollars a tube at drugstores—but can work wonders to soothe sore nipples. I used the stuff liberally with my first two babies, and it really helped. But with Will, my youngest, my lactation consultant told me that recently they've been finding that Polysporin (not Neosporin, but you can find it in the same section) is actually a stronger pain reliever and healer than Lansinoh. And it's a lot cheaper too. I asked my OB just to make sure this was a safe bet, and she confirmed that it's great for newly nursing moms.

One caveat: I always use a wet cloth to wipe down my nipples before feeding my baby, just to be supersafe and make sure there isn't extra cream residue on my nipples. I'm probably being overcautious—my lactation consultant and doctor both told me that the cream soaks in pretty quickly, making a wipe-down unnecessary—but when you're dealing with a new baby, I figure that even over-the-top neurosis like this is perfectly acceptable.

My last sore-nipple tip is to pick up a pack of Lansinoh Soothies (ten dollars at any drugstore). They are these little gel pads that are covered in lanolin. You put them in the fridge to make them all cold and then stick them in your bra after you get done feeding your baby. I'm telling you, it's like a mini spa treatment for your boobs. I'm talking a major "ahhh" factor for a sore, newly nursing mom. I've actually started buying these for all my friends when I go visit them with their new babies in the hospital. Sure, it's a little weird to give nipple pads to my friends as a gift, but once they try them, they all thank me.

Engorgement

The other major pain in your breasts (whether you breast-feed or not) is engorgement. Basically, for the first few days of your baby's life, your breasts will produce small quantities of foremilk, called *colostrum*. This yellow, thick milk is the perfect first food for your baby, as it's loaded with antibodies to protect your baby in her first few days of life, along with other cool things, like a laxative to help your baby expel meconium (his or her first poop) and prevent jaundice. It's all pretty incredible if you think about it.

After a few days, your baby will start to realize that the colostrum is not nearly enough to keep him satiated for more than seven minutes. And at that exact point, your body will recognize that it also needs to kick up its milk production and will start producing regular old breast milk. But this isn't a gradual process.

For me, I was sleeping peacefully one night when my son was about three days old and rolled over to get comfortable and bumped my breast against the mattress. I screamed. Not only were my boobs about five times larger than they had been when I went to bed the night before, but I wouldn't have been surprised had they burst like water balloons. They were warm and sore and throbbing. And, to top it all off, they were squirting milk out of them at a rate of approximately four cups per minute. (I didn't measure or anything, but since new moms are never prone to exaggeration, I'm sure that's somewhat accurate.) I literally squirted my husband in the face when I took off my shirt to try to get a look at them. Seriously.

Anyway, you will get engorged as your breasts adjust to producing milk. The good news is that after a few days, they'll become experts at gauging just how much your baby needs and adjusting production to fit those needs. (Again, incredible, right?) In the meantime, the best thing you can do is feed your baby as often as possible and if your baby isn't awake or wanting to suckle, use your hand or a breast pump on its lowest setting to express a small amount of milk (so you don't damage the already-sensitive breast tissue or put your milk-producing glands into overdrive, as the more you pump, the more you'll produce).

(Side note: if you're not planning to breast-feed, you'll still get engorged on approximately the second day of your baby's life and can use the same treatments to relieve the engorgement as you would during weaning.)

If you're not getting enough relief from breast-feeding or pumping (or if you've chosen not to breast-feed your baby and are trying to wean), there are some ways to relieve engorgement. The old wives swear by cabbage leaves. The strategy is to put a big, cold leaf of cabbage inside your bra every couple of hours and the chemical properties of the cabbage will decrease engorgement. I tried this when I weaned my first son, and the difference wasn't significant, although it did feel nice to have something cool pressed against my breasts. You can also try using cold (not warm or hot) compresses or gentle massage to relieve the pain and throbbing.

Another annoying part of engorgement is that your nipples need some time to learn to release milk at appropriate times (say, when your baby is eating) and not at inappropriate times (say, when you're walking into church). For the first few months, you may find that your nipples tend to leak a little. And by leak a little, I mean that anytime your baby (or anyone else's baby) cries or makes a noise, your nipples will take that to mean it's feeding time and immediately start squirting out milk, causing you to have two dark, wet spots on the front of your shirt. Embarrassing, right?

The simple solution to preventing this is to wear breast pads in your bra until your body has adjusted. You can buy disposable breast pads (my sister and I have affectionately named them "boob maxis") at a drugstore. These are little cotton disks that you slip into your bra and then remove and toss when you go to bed each night. The other option is washable breast pads—usually made from soft cotton or wool—that you can slip in your bra and then wash in the washing machine.

Postpartum Sex

Your Six-Week Postpartum Appointment

Right as your Christian Mama–style lying-in period comes to an end, your doctor or midwife will probably want you to come in for a final checkup to make sure everything is healing as it should. Now, your husband will probably offer to come along to this appointment with you, feigning an interest in how your body is healing after childbirth. But the truth is that he's going along for one reason and one reason alone: he wants to find out when the doctor will give you the go-ahead to have sex again. The conversation usually goes something like this:

DOCTOR: How are you feeling?

YOU: Great! Feeling almost back to normal.

YOUR HUSBAND: Yep, almost back to normal. Meaning, I think she's ready to—

DOCTOR [*interrupting your husband*]: Yep, she's completely ready to start going to spin class at the gym again.

YOUR HUSBAND: Oh, I meant, is she ready to … to …

DOCTOR: Oh, she doesn't spin? You're such a concerned husband! Of course she's released to do any and all kinds of exercise, as long as she doesn't push it too hard, too fast.

YOUR HUSBAND: So does that mean she's cleared to have sex?

DOCTOR: Oh, wow. No one has ever asked me that before! [*Winks at you.*] I'm not sure. Let me check the medical guides and get back to you.

Anyway, aside from some ribbing for your husband and some reassurance for you that everything down there has pretty much been restored to its normal order, this appointment is pretty straightforward. Your doctor or midwife will check your breasts, your tear, your C-section incision, and anywhere else that was affected by pregnancy, and then will probably do a Pap smear just to round out your obstetrical experience. After that, you'll be given the full clearance to leave your lying-in period, and you'll be turned loose on the world as a regular old gynecology patient again. Until your next pregnancy, at least.

Getting to the Good Stuff

Now, since your husband is probably reading over your shoulder at this point, mumbling something about how cruel it is to broach the subject of postpartum sex without actually giving any specific details, I'd be remiss if I didn't at least give you the basics. But before I do that, let me make one thing clear: every woman is different. Your postpartum healing will vary. And with that in mind there is no hard-and-fast number of days that it takes to be ready to have sex after having a baby. This is something you need to discuss with—you guessed it—your doctor or midwife, as well as your husband—before doing anything.

All that said, as a general rule, most women are cleared to have sex at their six-week appointment. At that visit, your doctor will check to make sure that any tearing you had has healed enough to ensure you won't get an infection, as well as make sure your body has healed enough to handle sex.

Of course, being cleared physically to have sex has no correlation to your emotional ability to handle sex. Most of my friends have admitted to having a paralyzing fear of postpartum sex—especially the first time. There's just something about the thought of touching the part of your body that was so traumatized that makes many women start to panic. So if you're feeling terrified of having sex—even if your doctor has cleared you—you may want to have a discussion with your husband about your fears. Here are some tips to get you over that hump (ha!).

Tips to Help Make Postpartum Sex Fun Instead of Frightening

1. **Give your hormones a talking-to**. After I had my babies, my hormones told me I never wanted to have sex ever, ever again, no matter what. This was a combination of fear (again, with the healing) and the fact that my hormones had completely stripped me of my sex drive and put me in mommy mode. But even while my body was saying no, I had to give my hormones a little lecture about how important physical intimacy is in building a strong marriage. And then I reminded them how much I would enjoy said intimacy if I just did it.
2. **Foreplay is your friend**. This is not a time for a quickie. Instead, ramp up to sex with a long bath, a back rub, a glass of wine (remember: two hours before nursing!) or a good ole make-out session on the couch. Give your body some time to remember how much fun it is to just be with your husband.
3. **Lubricant is also your friend**. You know those hormones that have wreaked havoc on your sex drive (see #1)? Well,

they really go all out with postpartum women, because they also cause vaginal dryness. This isn't a permanent thing, but for the first few months postpartum, you may want to pick up a tube of lube and use it liberally.

4. **Communicate how you're feeling**. It may feel weird or even embarrassing to explain your feelings—and the hormonal mayhem—to your husband. But you guys are a team, which means he can and will help you walk through this. Tell him what's going on, and reassure him that it's not him or your lack of desire, but it's simply something that happens after you have a baby.

5. **Get some tummy-hiding lingerie**. Your husband thinks you are absolutely beautiful, tummy flab and stretch marks and all. You can go ahead and take my word on that. But if you're anything like me, your body confidence is probably at an all-time low right after you have a baby. So for your sake—not his—pick up some lingerie that will be forgiving of all your postpartum flaws so you can focus on what really matters—building intimacy.

6. **Make sure your baby isn't in the room**. Many parents—myself included—let their babies sleep in their bedrooms in a bassinet or co-sleeper for the first few months. And while this is great for helping you bond with your baby, it's not exactly conducive to bonding with your husband. So I recommend finding another place to have sex while your baby is sleeping in your room. Use this as an excuse to explore the many fun places to have sex in your house or move the bassinet into the hallway for a few minutes so you can have some time to yourselves.

Taking Care of Yourself, Taking Care of Baby

Now that I've given you the nitty-gritty details about how to take care of yourself after you've had a baby, I probably need to tell you how to take care of your baby. And as a freebie bonus for buying this book, I'm giving you free tuition to my critically acclaimed Newborns 101 course (my sisters give me rave reviews). And best of all, the course is all included right here in this book so you won't even have to lug a heavy backpack across campus to attend! Let's get started.

THREE

Newborns 101

How to Care for Your Little Bundle

Newborns 101 Course Syllabus
Professor Erin MacPherson

Welcome to Newborns 101, the course where you'll learn everything you need to know to raise a healthy, happy, and (somewhat) clean baby. Failure is not an option—mostly because if you can't master diaper basics, you'll probably never be able to leave the house. So it's time to hunker down and get serious. Yes, there will be a final exam.

Course Objectives:

- To figure out how to change your baby's diaper without him peeing all over you, his changing table, and the $328 vintage dry-clean–only quilt you hung on his wall "just as a decoration."
- Creating a schedule that will allow your baby to wear each

of the 594 outfits she got at her baby shower—even if it's only long enough to take a picture.

- Impeccably timing your baby's first bath pictures to coincide with the end of baby acne.

Course Outline:

Section 1: Am I Really Competent Enough to Do This?
Section 2: The Giant, Hungry-Yet-Exhausted Elephant in the Room
Section 3: Newborn Basics
Section 4: The Newborn Nasties
Section 5: Fingernails and Toenails (aka "Baby Razors")

Section 1: Am I Really Competent Enough to Do This?

Hi, I'm Erin, and I'll be your professor for this course. Okay, so I don't have tenure (yet), but that's mostly because I don't technically work for a university (minor details). That said, I am a regular expert on baby care. I have three kids. And all three of my kids were newborns at one point. And, to put that in layman's terms, I have changed approximately 16,425 diapers (yes, I looked it up on Google), taken care of three belly button stumps, trimmed 794 fingernails, and managed to destroy 16 super-expensive white baby outfits with my inadequate understanding of how to use OxiClean.

But I wasn't always the newborn care expert that I am today. When the hospital decided to send me home—with just my husband as a backup—with my son Joey, I'm not afraid to admit that I was slightly unprepared to be trusted with his care. And by slightly unprepared, I mean that I was a terrified mess who wanted to camp out in the maternity ward until I could convince one of the nurses to take a job as a live-in (unpaid) newborn care consultant at my house. And since none of them wanted the job (go figure), I had to find out how to take care of my baby all on my own. And look at me now: I'm a bone fide professor of advanced newborn care. Sort of.

But take it from the girl who had never changed a diaper in her entire life when she had her first baby—things like changing diapers and trimming (aka nibbling) your baby's fingernails are not as hard as they may seem. This may come as a shock to you, but people have been taking care of newborns for thousands of years. And—get this—even before Google was invented to answer new moms' desperate middle-of-the-night questions about whether a loose-ish-looking umbilical cord stump is reason for concern (it's not), babies survived and thrived.

So before you call your mother-in-law to see if she wants to live with you for the next seventeen weeks until you can figure it out, let me reassure you that you can do this. You'll do great. And look at you, taking the first step to being a baby-care whiz kid already by enrolling in this course. So go grab your #2 pencils and a notepad and get ready to study hard, because as I said before, there is a final exam.

Section 2: The Giant, Hungry-Yet-Exhausted Elephant in the Room

Now, before I go any further into this chapter, I think I need to address the giant elephant in the room—you know: the one that's standing over there in the corner, demanding to be fed every twelve minutes and then staying up all night, screaming and crying, so you're an insane and blubbering mess who can hardly function enough to even think about things like taking an intensive course like this one on newborn care.

I get it. Making sure your baby is eating and sleeping is your number one priority right now. And if we're being honest, you're probably not going to be able to think clearly enough to pass any sort of final exam until you've mastered those two subjects. So I'm giving you my official permission to bookmark this page and thumb ahead to chapter 3, where you'll learn all about newborn sleep patterns, and chapter 4, where you'll learn all about feeding your baby. Go. Read them now. And once you've mastered those topics enough to at least be somewhat coherent, come back to this chapter. We can wait. We have all night.

Section 3: Newborn Basics

You know that time in health class when you had to take a baby doll home and take care of it for three days, changing its diaper every time a little buzzer beeped and feeding it every time a different alarm rang? Forget everything you learned in that little exercise. Because while you probably learned a lot about how to selectively tune out various types of beeping alarms, you most likely learned nothing about how to care for a newborn. Because—get this—newborns aren't dolls. They're real people. Shocking, right?

Here's something else: your baby is different from every single other baby that God has ever created in the history of the world. Completely unique. Completely individual. Completely yours. I think that's pretty awesome—we have one amazing God!—but I also think it can serve as a bit of reassurance. Because instead of frantically asking Mr. Google at two in the morning how to soothe your crying newborn, you can say a quick prayer and then trust that the God who knit your baby together bit by precious bit is also the God who understands exactly what your baby needs at this moment.

. . . .

Time-Out for Mom

For When You're Just Figuring Things Out

"Have I not commanded you? Be strong and courageous. Do not be afraid; do not be discouraged, for the LORD your God will be with you wherever you go." (Joshua 1:9)

My God of hope, I have nothing to fear as I walk through this life, because You are with me. You are with me when I am exhausted. You are with me when I'm stressed. You are with me when I am joyful. You are with me when I'm uncertain about what to do. And Lord, I pray that through Your strength, I am strong and courageous today and every day that follows. Thank You for the comfort of knowing that no matter what I face, You are by my side. Amen.

. . . .

Five Ways to Get an A+ in Newborn Care

1. **Hold your baby**. A lot. The idea that holding your baby will spoil him is about as accurate as the idea that the cookie diet will help you lose those last ten pounds of baby weight. So spend a lot of time holding your baby—not only when he is nursing or trying to go to sleep, but throughout the day as you go about your normal tasks.

2. **Get to know your baby**. When you were first married, you probably spent some time trying to figure out how to make your husband smile—a cute little smooch, a fresh batch of chocolate chip cookies, wearing that (sort-of) revealing V-neck when he came home from work. In the same way, try to figure out what makes your baby tick—whether it's a little hand massage or steady access to his milk jugs. That way, you can anticipate his needs and do that little booty-shakin' dance that makes him laugh *before* he starts to fuss. (Come to think of it, that booty-shakin' thing might work to keep both your baby *and* your husband happy.)

3. **Have an arsenal of baby soothers written in Sharpie on your arm**. The fact that your baby is too young to eat Dove chocolate by the handful when he's feeling anxious, coupled

with the fact that self-soothing is a trick that goes beyond a newborn's skill set, means that he may need some help calming down when he gets upset. Once you know what works for your baby, write it in Sharpie on your arm so you can refer back. Or, if you want to be all parent-ish, you could just hang a list up on your refrigerator. Here are some ideas:

- Play some music.
- Go outside or into another room to give him a change of scenery.
- Say, "*Shh, shh, shh*" over and over, like your mom used to do.
- Give your baby a little foot or back massage.
- Leave him alone for a few minutes. Perhaps he just needs to get away from all the stimulus around him. (Or he just needs a break from you. Kidding!)
- Dry your hair or run your vacuum cleaner to see if white noise will do the trick.
- Nurse him—even if he just ate. Some babies just like to use their mom's breast as a pacifier—and in my totally unprofessional (and slightly hippie) opinion, that's just fine.
- Rock him. Either in a baby rocker or in a baby swing.
- Go on a walk.
- Go on a car ride.
- Bounce up and down. (If your thighs get tired, just grin and bear it and remember that there's no-pain-no-gain when it comes to soothing your baby. That, or you could pick up a baby bouncer for twenty bucks at the baby store.)
- Sway back and forth, back and forth. Bonus points if you hold a lighter in the air and sing "Wonderful Tonight" at the top of your lungs.
- Let your husband—or Grandpa—try.
- Give your baby a pacifier.

4. **Take some breaks**. When Mama ain't happy, well, even the littlest members of the household will probably start protesting whatever it is that is making you upset (as a show of solidarity, of course) by crying, fussing, or whining. And while this doesn't typically go away after the newborn stage (or after the baby stage or toddler stage either), you can get a handle on this early on by allowing yourself some mommy-only time whenever you start to feel that you've had enough.

5. **Know that love really is (almost) enough**. Babies really are pretty undemanding (laugh now, but you'll totally agree with me in two years). They need to sleep. They need to eat. And they occasionally need a fresh diaper and a clothing change. Once you've taken care of those three things, all you really need to do is heap your sappy, you're-the-cutest-little-coochie-coochie-coo-ever love on them and you're set.

Section 4: The Newborn Nasties

Have you noticed how all of those icky, gross things like dirty diapers, spit-up, and drool become mere nuisances (and cute nuisances to boot) when your baby is doing them? Before, it was "Ew!" but now that it's your baby doing it, it's become, "Aw, look. She just did a little spitty." But all newborns—even your totally adorable little schnookums—have some nasty little ailments that show up in the first few months of life. Here's what to expect.

1. **Spit-up**. Most (if not all) babies spit up from time to time. It has something to do with gas bubbles in their immature digestive system that sometimes make everything flow backward instead of forward. (How's that for a technical definition?) Basically, that means that even if it seems as if your baby spits up every twelve minutes, it's probably perfectly normal. Of course, if you are concerned—or if you notice projectile vomiting (more on that in chapter 9 if you want details) call your doctor.

2. **Baby acne**. Somewhere around the two-week-old mark, most babies develop a very bad case of acne. (Think, your hormonal teen years meet that time you got forty-nine mosquito bites while hanging out at the lake.) This is—you guessed it— totally normal. That said, don't do something crazy, like use an apricot scrub or book a session with the dermatologist, because most of the time, it'll just go away on its own after a week or two. And whatever you do, resist the urge to pop those little whiteheads.

3. **Cradle cap**. If you notice hard, yellow patches on your baby's head (kind of like someone smeared peanut butter on her head and it hardened), it's probably cradle cap. It's completely harmless and it'll probably go away before her first birthday. If it's really bugging you, the old wives say you can rub olive oil on your baby's head and massage the patches to get them off.

4. **Drool**. Your baby—smart as she is—hasn't mastered the skill of closing her lips enough to keep her saliva inside her mouth. So instead of swallowing all that spit, she just lets it drip out—onto your shirt, onto her sheets, onto everything. Fun. The good news is that most kids master this skill before they turn one—and if they don't, they'll certainly figure it out before you resort to sending them to school wearing a bib.

Section 5: Fingernails and Toenails (aka "Baby Razors")

I have some unresolved trauma based on a nail-clipping incident that happened in early 2006. The day had started out like any other day. I had awakened at 4:42 a.m. to the wailing of my three-week-old son Joey, who seemed to think that 4:42 a.m. was a perfectly acceptable time for a snack. I proceeded to feed him and then drink two and a half cups of decaf while I bounced on the giant exercise ball in the living room and tried to get him to go back to sleep so I could at least nab a catnap before the day began.

And, in the midst of all that normalcy, I had the brilliant idea that perhaps I should cut Joey's razor-sharp fingernails so he wouldn't claw himself in the face during his next nap. So I went upstairs and got out the handy-dandy baby-care kit and pulled out the safety clippers that my friends had all sworn worked "perfectly" and "were so easy to use that even a bleary-eyed new mom could figure them out" and started clipping.

Perhaps it was the fact that my hands were shaking from the decaf or maybe it was the fact that Joey's nails were so tiny that I couldn't even tell if he had nails, much less see where the nails ended and the skin began, but I cut him. And he cried. For, like, three minutes. And even today—almost six years later—he is still traumatized about having me cut his nails. Okay, so maybe it's the other way around. Maybe I'm the one who adamantly refuses to go near my kids' hands with nail clippers and makes them wait until Daddy gets home if they happen to break a nail.

Anyway, I digress. Newborn fingernails and toenails are tiny. Like, tiny-tiny. Like, so tiny that even if you had a magnifying glass and a headlamp on, you're unlikely to be able to gauge exactly where the nail is in order to clip it without accidentally clipping your baby's skin from time to time. So, I say don't do it. Save those fancy baby clippers until your baby is four months old (or in my case, fourteen) and just use a soft fingernail file to smooth the rough and sharp edges. Or my friend Barb told me that she just bit her son's nails while he was breast-feeding. A little nibble here, a little nibble there, and by the time he was done, his nails were smooth and short. I've never tried that one—for some reason the idea of biting anyone's nails kind of grosses me out—but hey, if it works, why not? Better than being traumatized by seeing blood gushing (okay, dripping in tiny drops) off of your newborn's hand.

Extra Credit Section: The Umbilical Cord

This section of our course is extra credit. It's your special little bonus just for taking the class. Why? Because you don't have to do a single thing. Yep, that's right. All you have to do is leave your baby's umbilical cord alone until the stub falls off and you'll get fifty bonus points as well as your pediatrician's undying love and respect.

Now, wait, you're probably thinking. *My great-aunt's cousin's best friend told me that I have to rub my baby's umbilical cord with special alcohol swabs every four hours for the first seventeen and a half days of her life. Oh, and my mom told me that I should use Vaseline to make it soft and pliable so it would come off easier.* I know, I know. I did all those things with my first two babies' umbilical cords too. I rubbed those stubs with alcohol swabs like clockwork for weeks and weeks.

But then I had my youngest, Will. And my pediatrician told me that all that alcohol swabbing and Vaseline rubbing was actually unnecessary. In fact, an umbilical cord stub does best if you just leave it alone. Don't touch it. Don't wiggle it. Don't rub it or clean it or spray it. Don't even look at it if you don't want. Just leave it alone. See? The easiest part of this entire class.

One caveat: umbilical cord stubs really shouldn't get wet if at all possible. So, while it's perfectly fine to give your baby a sponge bath starting on day one, it's probably best to wait until the stub falls off for one of those fully submerged tub baths that garner all those great photo ops.

The Final Exam

You've done it! You've mastered the basics, read the requirements, taken careful notes, and you, my students, are ready to be turned loose into the world as official graduates of the school of newborn care.

Of course, there is the small issue of the final exam to take care of before you don your cap and gown. And in an effort to make sure you demonstrate complete mastery of the subject, I've decided that this exam must be not only comprehensive, but also lab-based. That's right; you're going to have to put your newfound skills into action. So grab your baby and your notes and get started. From this point forward, you are officially in charge of taking care of your baby's every need—every diaper change, every cry, every everything.

Wait—you're already doing that? Never mind then. I guess I just need to start handing out diplomas.

FOUR

Lovin' Your Lil' Night Owl

How to Get Your Baby to Sleep

I f your baby is anything like my daughter, she probably equates the sun going down with an invitation to *par-tay*. And of course, your baby doesn't want to par-tay alone in her crib! She wants company. And speaking of company—she doesn't want just *any* company—she really just wants *you* and your fully stocked milk bar to join her. And since you love your baby more than anything (and it's pretty hard to sleep when she's screaming her lungs out), you've suddenly become very adept at functioning on 2.3 hours of interrupted sleep per night.

At this point, you probably don't care about bonding or spit-up or baths or even about that cute little baby poncho your sister-in-law just found on Etsy.com. Right now, you care about one thing and one thing only: sleep. And it's no wonder. How can any formerly self-sufficient adult be expected to function when she isn't sleeping?

The good news is that the never-sleep-ever-ever phase is short-lived. I know; you don't want to hear that, but it is. Even the worst-sleeping babies (read: my daughter) eventually start sleeping. And when it happens, you'll develop a very severe case of sleep-deprived amnesia where you'll swear to other desperate new moms that it really wasn't *that* bad and that you'd do it again in a second. Just warning you.

But until then, I thought I'd take a crack at the old sleep-advice game. After all, everyone and their mother is giving it. Sleep "experts" are everywhere. Friends. Family. Neighbors. Women in line at the grocery store. Everyone is a treasure trove of sleeping advice—and *everyone* knows exactly what you need to get your baby sleeping.

You hear advice in the grocery store: "Three months, eh? Oh, my baby had been sleeping through the night for *weeks* at that age."

You hear advice at church: "Don't you dare let that baby cry. Even for a minute! This, too, shall pass! Sleep is overrated anyway."

I have a confession to make. I used to be *that* mom. I thought I was pretty darn good at the whole sleep-training thing, and since I was so proficient, I figured I should probably share my expertise with anyone and everyone who asked. Or didn't ask but looked like they wanted my advice. You see, my firstborn, Joey, was a great sleeper from day one. And since he was such a fabulous sleeper, I figured that my parenting skills had to have played a role in it. It certainly wasn't that he was just naturally a good sleeper. No. It was me—I was a sleep-training genius! Or so I thought.

Fast-forward two years and I had my daughter. Of course, since I was such a great sleep trainer, I assumed she'd also be a great sleeper. And, of course, I was wrong. My daughter was a terrible sleeper. She absolutely refused to sleep in her crib. Or at night. Or to go more than two hours without breast-feeding. And suddenly, I was that mom standing in line at the grocery store with the dark circles under her eyes and that desperate-for-help look.

Just as suddenly, I was now the recipient of lots of off-the-cuff sleep advice. Moms everywhere were giving me that pitying glace and telling me how they managed to sleep train their kids. And while those well-meaning moms often had great advice—more often than not, it was advice that didn't work for my impossible-to-sleep-train daughter.

God created your baby to be a fabulously unique person with a personality (and sleep habits) to prove it. The key to getting some shut-eye is figuring out exactly what will work for your baby—and making that work for you. Here's how to get started.

So, Really, How Do I Get This Kid to Sleep?

I know you're tired. Really tired. And I know you'd like nothing more than for me to give you a definite, tried-and-true method that will 100 percent guarantee that your baby is going to sleep through the night—preferably tonight. Sorry to be the bearer of bad news, but that's probably not going to happen. But maybe soon. All you have to do is invent your very own personalized sleep training method.

Um, yeah. You'll get right on that, right? Right after you go on your morning jog (ha!) and scrub those toilets that you haven't touched since before you got pregnant. No, really. It's not *that* hard. I'm not asking you to write a book or solve the quadratic equation (you already did that in high school, *thankyouverymuch*), but simply to think about your baby and what makes him tick. The main reason there are so many sleep books—all of which promise to be the absolute perfect solution for you and your baby—is that there are so many babies. You already know that God made each child to be a completely unique person with his or her own personality—but what you may not have thought of (you're sleep deprived; no one blames you) is that those tried-and-true solutions that work perfectly for some babies may not work for *your* baby.

With my son I was very successful with the Oblivious Shower Method. Basically, I read my son a book. I nursed him. I sang "Jesus

Loves Me." I rubbed his little back. Then I set him in his crib, gave him one last kiss, and hightailed it out of there before he realized I was gone. From there, I hopped in the shower and washed all of the day's spit-up off my neck, and by the time I went back in to check on him, he was almost always sound asleep.

My daughter wasn't so easy. The Oblivious Shower Method only resulted in my having to get out of the shower before I rinsed out the conditioner because I could hear my daughter's screams over the sound of the water. I tried everything. I tried rocking her. I tried singing. I tried white noise. I tried shushing her. I tried Ferberizing and Weissbluthizing and Pantley-izing (if you don't know what I'm talking about, you soon will) and all to no avail. My daughter simply did *not* want to sleep.

In the end, I did what any desperate-for-sleep mom would do: I let her sleep in my bed with me. And anytime she started crying, I simply rolled over, popped my boob into her mouth, and fell back asleep while she nursed. I confess: I used the put-a-boob-in-her-mouth-and-hope-it-works approach with her for way, way too long. You can only imagine what a blast it was to sleep train her when we finally decided to put the kibosh on the breast-feeding-all-night thing and make her sleep in her crib. (Disclaimer: Sleeping with your baby—especially without a co-sleeper or snuggle nest—can be dangerous. So, while desperate times can call for desperate measures, you should probably talk to your pediatrician before trying this.)

Eventually we did sleep train Kate—she's a great sleeper now. The trick was coming up with our very own (and very personalized) sleep training method for her. None of the stuff that had worked for other babies worked for my daughter, so I had to invent my own method. Now, I know you're tired and cranky and really don't feel like inventing anything at all—but this is worth it. It will make you the ultimate superstar in your household after you simultaneously find the solution to household peace and regain the energy you need to cook dinner in one fell swoop. So put your thinking cap on—and I'm going to make this really, really easy for you. Here's my step-by-step guide on how to invent your own personal sleep training method.

Inventing Your Very Own
Sleep Training Method

Step One: Watch your baby.

That's easy. You're already doing that. Like 24/7, right? But now, you need to watch your baby with a purpose. Does he seem to calm down when you swaddle him? Or does he get all droopy-eyed when you rub his back and sing to him? Does your baby seem to settle in when he hears the noise of the vacuum cleaner? Spend a few days honing in on what makes your baby tick—and what makes your baby head straight to zzz-land. If you happen to be able to find a piece of paper and a pen, you may want to jot a few things down, just so you don't forget.

Step Two: Keep a sleep log.

Okay, so this isn't my idea. I have to give credit to Kim West and Marc Weissbluth and about every other sleep expert who has ever written a book or claimed to know what they are talking about when it comes to sleep. There is one thing that nearly every sleep expert agrees on: if you want to get your baby to sleep, you first have to figure out your baby's natural sleep patterns.

Some sleep experts recommend that you get a fancy journal or notebook from the store, but that would require you to (a) leave the house, and (b) manage to find the notebook section of the store before your baby starts crying. With that in mind, I personally recommend that you simply swipe a piece of plain white computer paper out of your printer. On it, keep track of every time your baby falls asleep and wakes up for an entire week. Every nap. Every bedtime. Every faked-you-out-by-falling-asleep-for-five-minutes-at-bedtime-before-I-start-crying-again incident.

Step 3: Come up with a plan.

This is the part that will take some thinking power—which means you may want to brew yourself a really big pot of coffee so you can focus. Once you have your coffee in hand, take out your sleep log and see if you can find some patterns. Does your baby tend to fall asleep around 9:00 a.m. right after breakfast? Does he get really fussy around 8:00 p.m. every night? Does he always fall asleep in the car when you run errands after lunch? These are your baby's natural sleep patterns—which means those are the times when your baby will most naturally fall asleep without crying.

After months of moaning and groaning about the fact that my daughter never, ever slept, I finally decided to try keeping a sleep log. After a few days of recording, I saw some definite patterns emerging. My daughter always got sleepy and started to rub her eyes right after I fed my son breakfast (which, by the way, was right when my son wanted to play). She also seemed to fall asleep about twenty minutes after I gave her a bath—regardless of whether her bath was mid-morning or late at night.

With that in mind, I made a sleep schedule. I planned her morning nap for 9:00 a.m. I planned her afternoon nap for 2:00 p.m. At night I created a bedtime routine that involved a warm bath and then twenty minutes of singing, stories, and prayer before finally tucking her into her crib. Guess what? It worked. Not right away, but after a few weeks of sticking to our routine, my daughter was actually sleeping. In her crib.

You can do the same thing. The key is to make it very personal for your baby. If your baby falls asleep to the sound of the fan whirring, put it on high before you tuck him in. If your baby seems to drift off every time U2 comes on the iPod, start blaring it in his room at night.

Step 4: Stick to your plan.

Once you have a plan, stay with it and give it some time to work. You know that whole thing where they say it takes 4,234 (or some number like that) repetitions of something to form a habit? Well, your baby needs to get into the sleeping habit. So if your whole bath, song, listen-to-U2 routine doesn't work at first, don't throw the baby out with the bathwater. (Or, the bath out with the baby water. Whatever.) You need to give your plan a good two or three weeks to work—and be patient when you hit little setbacks.

Step 5: Adjust your plan.

I know I just told you to stick to your plan, but after three weeks or so, if the plan still isn't doing anything to improve upon the sleeping situation at your house, you can go ahead and assume that your plan isn't right and start over at step one (yes, step one!). I can't guarantee that my little sleep method will work on all babies (after all, like I said, every baby is different), but it's worth a try, right? What do you have to lose?

8 Ways to Soothe Your Baby to Sleep

When it's 3:00 a.m. and you've been pacing the floor with a screaming baby in your arms for four hours, you'll do pretty much anything to get that baby to sleep—even if it means standing next to your baby's crib with your finger in your baby's mouth for two hours. Here are a few things to try during those desperate moments—at the very least, you'll have something to divert your attention from your middle-of-the-night desperation.

1. **White noise.** Whether it's the vacuum, the seashore noise from a white noise player, or the sound of a fan running at high power, muted, repetitive noise is apparently comforting to babies because they heard a lot of shushing and whooshing and whirring when they were in your uterus. And here you thought your baby was spending her time listening to that "prenatal education" CD you bought.

2. **Adjust the light.** Some babies need a room to be pitch-black

in order to sleep. Others like bright sunlight. After spending seventy bucks on blackout shades for my son's nursery, I figured out that he slept better when the room had some natural light.

3. **Get some (soft) music**. A lot of babies love music playing on the CD player. When my son was a baby, I was in a Norah Jones phase, so I popped her latest CD into his CD player and he drifted right off to sleep. When my husband got home, he made me take the CD out right away. Apparently he considers Norah "sex music." Who knew?

4. **Try bouncing**. Get one of those exercise balls (they're in that rarely visited exercise section at Target or Wal-Mart) and try sitting on one while bouncing your baby. And yes, bouncing on the ball while trying to get your baby to sleep totally counts as a workout.

5. **Take some clothes off**. It's a mom thing to try to bundle your baby in the warmest-ever pajamas for bedtime—but counterintuitive as it sounds, babies actually tend to sleep better when they are wearing cool, breathable clothes.

6. **Leave the room**. I know, you don't want to leave the poor little thing all *alone*, but sometimes just being near you—well, you and your milk jugs—can be a bit overstimulating for your baby.

7. **Give him a little top-off**. Okay, so some sleep experts say that it's not a good idea to feed your baby to sleep, but, like bribery, I'm not against the occasional top-off at night. Or in the day. Hey, if it gets your baby to sleep, it gets your baby to sleep.

8. **Change your baby's sleeping arrangement**. My nephew Jude hated his crib for the first few months of his life. But he loved his car seat. The second my sister-in-law would strap him in, he'd start snoozing. So, what did Stevi do? She plopped his car seat down in his crib each night and let him sleep in there. Brilliant.

Time-Out for Mom

For When You're Utterly Exhausted

"May your unfailing love be my comfort, according to your promise to your servant." (Psalm 119:76)

Everlasting God, Your love is unfailing! Even when I'm exhausted and overwhelmed and unable to think straight, You comfort me with a love that goes beyond human understanding. God, today, fill me with that love so that regardless of my emotions, my hormones, and my lack of sleep, I am fully aware of the comfort that comes from knowing I am loved by my almighty God. Amen.

· ·

The Sleep Books Rundown

To be completely honest, the whole idea of reading a book to learn how to lull your baby to sleep (and therefore catch some zzz's yourself) is inherently illogical. Because the reality is that if you happen to find yourself in a situation where (a) your baby is sleeping, and (b) you've already taken care of all urgent life matters like using the restroom and taking a shower, then you should probably spend your time actually sleeping instead of reading a book about sleeping.

But I digress. I've read most (if not all) of the sleep books known to motherhood, and despite the fact that I probably should've been napping instead of reading, I actually enjoyed most of them. I found the tips helpful, the advice sound, and I actually used a lot of the strategies and ideas in creating my own kids' sleep plans. But since I've already done all of the hard work, I'll make it easy for you. Here's a list of the most popular sleep-training books and a quick rundown on what they're about.

1. *Healthy Sleep Habits, Happy Child* by Dr. Marc Weissbluth

The gist: One size does not fit all, according to Dr. Weissbluth, who analyzes everything from differences between daytime naps and nighttime sleep to the differences between a sleepy baby and an active toddler. From there, he gives you suggestions to encourage your baby's natural sleep rhythms so she will fall asleep according to her own internal clock.

The pros: Instead of assuming that we live in a world of cookie-cutter babies, Weissbluth knows that your baby is fabulously unique. That means if you have a baby who always falls asleep when you turn on the Food Network, he'll have a solution for that.

The cons: Weissbluth's book focuses on many ages and stages, so if you're only wanting to know about newborn sleep (duh), you'll have to skip around a bit.

2. *The Happiest Baby on the Block* by Dr. Harvey Karp

The gist: Dr. Karp believes that the first three months after birth should actually be thought of as the fourth trimester (which would explain why you still can't fit into anything besides maternity clothes). With this in mind, he believes that the outside world can be a bit disorienting to newborns, whom he considers to be in the fourth trimester—hence, the incessant crying and screaming. He recommends various calming techniques (like swaddling, singing, and *shh* sounds) that will resemble the uterus and help your baby feel calm and comfy enough to sleep.

The pros: Dr. Karp's plan is very soothing and tends to work really well for newborns, who are still adjusting to the world.

The cons: My friend Amanda, who swore by Dr. Karp's plan when her baby was a newborn, said that when her son hit four months, the shushing and swaddling didn't work anymore and she had to think of a new plan to get her son sleeping.

3. *The No-Cry Sleep Solution* by Elizabeth Pantley

The gist: Elizabeth Pantley encourages you to create a

customized, step-by-step sleep plan for your baby. Wait. Where have you heard that before? Yeah, I stole that idea from Pantley because it makes sense and it works. Additionally, Pantley also shows you various techniques for discovering your baby's natural biological rhythms so you can get some sleep without having to hear your baby cry for minutes (or hours!) on end.

The pros: For obvious reasons, if you can get your baby to sleep without crying, then everyone is happy.

The cons: Many babies just need to cry to get to sleep. Simple as that. My son was one of those babies. He always cried for about two minutes before he fell asleep, no matter what. I hated it. I could have the most elaborate sleep routine and put him in his crib half asleep and completely relaxed and he'd still rouse himself enough to cry it out for a few minutes before drifting off. With that in mind, don't expect the no-cry sleep solution to be the *right* solution for every baby.

4. *On Becoming Baby Wise* by Gary Ezzo and Robert Bucknam

The gist: Ezzo and Bucknam focus on a parent-centered household—meaning you actually get to decide when your baby sleeps and eats and all that jazz instead of letting a two-month-old tyrant control your every move. *Baby Wise* suggests that you put your baby on a (somewhat) strict feeding and sleeping schedule that will help him adjust to *your* routines instead of having the world adjust to his whims.

The pros: Your daily schedule isn't dictated by an unexpected nap or a sudden feeding, but instead, you're able to plan your time, your days, and (best of all) your nights. This program reports unbelievable success at getting babies to sleep through the night consistently and fairly early on.

The cons: There have been a few (very, very rare) reports of infant malnutrition when parents use this method. The reason is that babies are fed on a schedule instead of when they are hungry, and some babies—especially small newborns—need food more often than that. Also, since you are putting your baby on a sleeping routine, your baby will protest at first, meaning you'll have to suck it up and listen to your baby cry in her crib for a while until she gets used to the routine.

5. *Secrets of the Baby Whisperer* by Tracey Hogg and Melinda Blau

The gist: I'm a middle-ground kind of girl. There's no way I'm going to wait twenty minutes to feed my baby if she's screaming hysterically from hunger, but I also crave routine and love myself a good schedule. *Baby Whisperer*'s approach works for the middle-ground type of mom. Basically, when you're getting your baby on a schedule, you follow what Tracey Hogg calls "the E.A.S.Y method." First your baby *eats* (that's the *E*); then you do an *activity*, like tummy time or peekaboo (the *A*); then you put her to *sleep* (the *S*); then you run to the kitchen and pour yourself a huge cup of coffee and prance around, celebrating your success (the *Y* stands for *your time*). This gets your baby into an easy, workable routine and saves you from always feeding your baby to sleep.

The pros: *Baby Whisperer* provides a middle ground for moms who don't want a rigid schedule but also want some routine in their lives.

The cons: Keeping your baby from falling asleep during a middle-of-the-night (or pre-nap) feeding is next to impossible. Really. Try it.

6. *Solve Your Child's Sleep Problems* by Richard Ferber

The gist: Dr. Ferber is, like, the bona fide world guru on sleep training. In fact, if you walk into a room full of fifty been-there, done-that moms and said, "Ugh! I'm Ferberizing my baby right now," every single one of them would give you a pitying smile and say, "Hang in there; it'll get better." Yup. Ferberizing is synonymous with sleep training. And here's why: Ferber is the director of Boston's Center for Pediatric Sleep Disorders and has spent years and years studying sleep. With that expertise, he developed a system that involves letting your baby cry for short (but increasing) amounts of time in order to teach them to fall asleep on their own.

The pros: Like *On Becoming Baby Wise*, Ferber's plan works. Almost everyone I know who has tried his method reported at least some success. Even better, it often works pretty quickly.

The cons: Ferber's method does involve some crying. He doesn't say, "Throw your baby in her crib and let her cry all night, if that's what it takes," but he does have you leave a crying baby in her crib for increasing amounts of time. And not that I know this from experience or anything, but if you do, say, take your baby out of the crib in a moment of weakness, it kind of negates the process and makes it so your baby starts believing that if she cries hard enough, eventually you'll come. Just sayin'.

Sleep Gear

Remember when you were pregnant? How could you forget, right? Remember how whenever you walked into a baby store, the clerks honed in on you, certain that the very fact that you were pregnant meant that you absolutely needed at least one of every item in the store?

Well, now that you're a mom, you're not immune. Now, the clerks take one look at those bags under your eyes and instantly determine that you are (a) sleep deprived and (b) so desperate that you'll try (or buy) anything to get yourself some sleep. So what do you really need? Is the soothing lavender sleep lotion really worth your six bucks? And if you splurge on a "sleep guaranteed" lullaby CD, will your baby really be guaranteed sleep, like, tonight?

Here's my rundown on all the sleep gear out there—and, yes, I tried it all. It's not my fault! My daughter never, ever slept, and those salespeople are super-pushy.

Sleep Gear That You May (or May Not) Need
1. **Aromatherapy baby wash and lotion**. You're probably already an expert on aromatherapy (hellooo, scrumptious

vanilla massage cream), but in case you haven't been to Bath & Body Works in a while, let me fill you in. Certain scents—like lavender and vanilla—tend to be sleep-inducers. So if you're washing your baby in yummy-smelling soap that happens to help them relax, it can't hurt. To be honest, I tried this with my daughter, and it didn't seem to make a difference, but she smelled yummy, and the soap is the same price as the regular baby soap, so I figured it was worth it.

2. **A nap nanny**. This is a really, really snazzy, supersoft, raised-foam thing that cradles and snuggles your baby to sleep. I've actually never used one, because they weren't invented when my daughter was a baby, but my friend Sarah borrowed one from her friend and said it was a lifesaver. Her daughter fell asleep in it instantly. One caveat: it's a $129 lifesaver that your baby will only sleep in for three months, max. But if three months' worth of sleep is worth 129 smackaroos to you, then go for it.

3. **A sleep sack**. SIDS rules—which you should follow to the letter—say you shouldn't have anything in your baby's crib except for a light receiving blanket and your baby. Easy—except for the fact that when Joey got cold, he woke up. And when he woke up, it took me two hours of singing and bouncing and cooing to get him back to sleep. So I got him a sleep sack. A sleep sack is basically a wearable blanket that you can zip around your baby to keep him warm. They're pretty awesome—and if you live in a cold climate or if your husband cranks the AC down to just-below-freezing every night, like mine does, it's a pretty important thing to have.

4. **A sleep positioner**. You may or may not be able to find one of these in stores—most have been recalled—but just in case you get one handed down to you, I want to warn you that while a sleep positioner is a good idea in theory, they can be dangerous for babies. The point of a sleep positioner is to make it so once your baby is sleeping comfortably in one spot, he won't be able to wiggle-worm his way out of that spot. The

problem? Some babies were able to wiggle-worm just enough to get themselves caught facedown—causing a big SIDS risk. In sum, this is one thing you should not let yourself get talked into trying.

5. **A white noise maker**. My friend Stacy's daughter could only fall asleep to the sound of the vacuum cleaner running. So after vacuuming their house every day for two weeks straight, Stacy got smart and recorded the noise of the vacuum onto a CD and played it on repeat in her daughter's room. It worked like a charm. If your baby seems to be soothed by the sound of the fan whirring or the vacuum running, then you might want to pick up a white noise maker.

6. **A lullaby CD**. My son loved to have soft music playing when he fell asleep. At first I spent big bucks on expensive infant "sleep guaranteed" CDs—but then I got smart and realized that my son didn't care what kind of music was playing, as long as it was somewhat soft and slow. From there, I started playing old jazz favorites, like Nat King Cole and Frank Sinatra—music he still loves to this day.

7. **A swaddler**. Fact: you will never, ever be as good at swaddling your baby as the nurses in the hospital. They have had much more practice. But you can cheat and buy a Velcro swaddler. My sister and her husband called their Velcro swaddler their "special little baby straitjacket." Try it—even a rookie dad can get a squirmy and sobbing baby swaddled tightly and securely in five minutes or less.

How to Survive on Three Hours (or Less) of Sleep

1. **Sleep when your baby sleeps**. I know; you've heard that a million times, but it has to be your priority. That means if your baby goes down for a nap at 8:30 a.m., you do too. And if

your baby is in bed at 6:30 p.m., you'll have to TiVo *Survivor* and watch it at 2:00 a.m. when your baby is rarin' to go.

2. **Get some help**. Let your mom take the baby on a walk while you nap, or let your husband get up so you can sleep. Take any and every opportunity you can get to sleep.

3. **Lay off of the coffee**. I know it sounds counterintuitive for me to tell you not to drink coffee when you're sleep deprived, but having your system in caffeine overdrive will make it harder to fall asleep when you actually do get the chance. I suggest having one or two cups in the morning when your baby has just woken up from a nap and you know you'll be up for a few hours anyway. After that, switch to decaf or have some herbal tea.

4. **Cut back on screen time**. While it's totally fine to send (another) e-mail with (more) pictures of your baby to all of your friends, you may want to avoid spending hours and hours in front of the computer or TV. Too much artificial light can make it hard for you to fall asleep when you need to, and can make your eyes blurry (as if you weren't bleary-eyed enough already).

5. **Get out of the house**. Pop your baby in the stroller, and go on a long walk outside. Just don't push it too hard. The last thing you need is to be exhausted, sweaty, *and* sore all at the same time.

6. **Eat a healthy snack**. Instead of reaching for a sugar-high- (and then sugar-low-) inducing candy bar, reach for a healthy snack with protein, like crackers with peanut butter or a string cheese. No, it won't give the same rush that the sugar gives you, but you'll feel more awake and more alert for much longer.

This, Too, Shall Pass

Remember how I told you that my daughter, Kate, was the worst sleeper ever as a baby? She was. But guess what? She's a great sleeper now. In fact, she's upstairs sleeping soundly right now as I write this—and I didn't have to do anything crazy to get her to sleep. I just tucked her in and kissed her forehead. I'm not telling you this to make you jealous (although, I'm sure you just felt a twinge of envy) but simply to assure you that your sleepless nights won't last forever. All babies—even the worst of them—eventually start sleeping.

So, even if your baby is a genuine night owl who keeps you up until 2:00 a.m. and then wakes up rarin' to go at 4:30, it will pass. If he fusses all night and then coos all day, it will pass. And if he won't go to sleep unless the fan is on and you're snuggling against him, it will still (most likely) pass. You'll get there. And in the meantime, look on the bright side: at least you're very well informed on what's going on in the lives of Jay Leno and Craig Ferguson.

FIVE

Breast Assured

How to Breast-Feed (and Like It)

Those of you who have read my pregnancy book know I'm a huge advocate of breast-feeding. But allow me to let you in on a little secret: I wasn't always the card-holding, breast pump–carrying lactivist that I am now. In fact, before I had my first son, I wasn't even sure I was going to breast-feed. But then I tried it and I liked it. I had only had sore nipples for a few days. My baby latched on really well. I had no problem producing enough milk. And since it was really easy for me and it made my baby all sweet and snuggly and sleepy to boot, I jumped on the bandwagon wholeheartedly. And then I got all advocate-y about it.

I know I'm a rare exception. A lot of moms really struggle with breast-feeding. And I know that all moms love their babies dearly and desperately want to do what's best, and often that means feeding with formula or doing some sort of breast-and-bottle hybrid. And that's totally okay. In fact, it's more than okay. It means you're thinking clearly about what's best for you and your baby instead of doing what the nurses and lacta-tion consultants and people like me tell you to do.

So while I'm going to get all preachy about breast-feeding right now, I want to make it clear up front that I have no intention of shov-ing a Boppy in your face while ranting off totally untrue facts about how every child who is breast-fed automatically gets four hundred free bonus points on his SAT. Because the truth is that unless you decide to adopt the Hi-C-and-donut diet with your two-month-old (in which case I *will* judge you), your baby will be just fine. In fact, he will be better than fine: he's got you for a mommy, after all.

Reasons to Breast-Feed

As I told you before, I wasn't always a lactivist. In fact, when I was pregnant with my first baby, I was pretty ambivalent about it. But, as I studied and read about breast-feeding (here's the part where my lactivism comes out), I realized that the many benefits of breast-feeding outweighed the frustration, pain, and inconvenience. For me. So I'm a gung-ho breast-feeder. Here are my reasons:

1. **Breast milk is easiest for babies to digest**. Tiny babies have immature digestive systems (which is why that Hi-C-and-donut diet I mentioned earlier is such a bad idea)—so breast-feeding allows their digestive systems to practice digesting with the simplest, most easily digested food before they ramp up to more complex foods, like pureed peas and smooshed pears. There's also the added bonus that breast milk changes as your baby develops and grows to fit her needs. God thought of everything, didn't He?

2. **Breast milk helps keep your baby healthy**. I'm sure a doctor could give you a much more detailed explanation, but just in case you aren't friends with any immunologists on Facebook, I'll just tell you what my pediatrician told me: the antibodies in your body that have developed as you've been exposed to

and fought illnesses over the years seep into your breast milk and can play a part in protecting your baby from those same illnesses. And as someone who has spent a week in the NICU with a sick baby, I can tell you that any little thing you can do to protect your baby from getting sick is a good thing.

3. **Breast milk decreases your baby's risk of an allergic reaction**. In a world where kids are developing allergies at an alarming rate, I want to do everything in my power to protect my children from developing allergies. It is very rare for an infant to have an allergic reaction to breast milk, and breast-feeding also has been shown to reduce the risk of developing other allergies later on.

4. **Breast-feeding is convenient**. Okay, so anyone who is in the first two or three weeks of breast-feeding will tell you that breast-feeding is anything but convenient. But once you get the hang of it, it becomes really simple. Your milk supply is just there—so you never have to worry about mixing bottles at midnight, packing enough formula in your diaper bag or running to the store at 3:00 a.m. when you realize you just used your last scoop of formula.

5. **Breast-feeding is cheap**. Some people may argue that breast milk isn't entirely free because mom has to eat more calories to produce the milk, but even comparing apples to oranges, the cost of formula is exponentially higher. (I just looked on Amazon.com, and a thirty-four-ounce can of formula—which, according to the package, makes sixty-one 4-ounce bottles—costs thirty-eight bucks. Let's just say that you can buy a whole lot of drive-thru tacos with that kind of cash. And I'm all for anything that gives me a free pass to eat a little more myself.)

6. **It'll help with the baby weight**. I'll be the first to tell you that regardless of what your twenty-two-year-old cousin who has never weighed more than 112 pounds says, breast-feeding does not just make the baby weight melt away overnight. Trust me. I've breast-fed three babies, and it got harder each time to lose

the baby weight. But breast-feeding does burn calories—up to five hundred extra calories a day—and no matter how you do the math, burning an extra five hundred calories every day for sitting in a chair, holding your baby, can't be a bad thing.

7. **It protects your health**. I don't have many details on this, so you'll have to ask Mr. Google if you want to know more, but recent studies have shown that breast-feeding can increase a mom's bone strength—which helps prevent osteoporosis— as well as decrease her risk for breast, uterine, and ovarian cancers.

Reasons Not to Breast-Feed

Of course, the flip side to the whole breast-is-best debate is that there are many, many moms who simply can't breast-feed for one reason or another. And instead of rallying around these moms to support them as they make the best choice for their children, many people judge them, rant at them, and preach at them. And while there's a lot of research out there about how breast is best, the attitude that someone else could possibly know more about what's best for your family does nothing but divide mom against mom. And when you're a new mom, you need all the mama friends you can get.

Plus, if you really think about it, if you took a group of ten one-year-olds and lined them up at My Gym and had them perform various agility and mental function tasks (read: had them crawl on foam pillows and throw plastic balls), I doubt you could tell which babies were breast-fed and which were formula fed. Because the truth is that the type of milk your baby drinks really isn't that big of a factor in the long-term health and growth of your baby. It's just not.

My friend Nicole tried to breast-feed her son for six weeks— suffering through horrible cracked nipples, low milk supply, and an impossible latch situation (resulting from her son's tongue tie combined with her inverted nipples). It just wasn't working. But people kept telling her things like, "Just try harder; it'll get better" or, "You need to visit the right lactation consultant and you'll figure it out." And those comments, combined with her desperate desire to do what was best for her son, resulted in her trying to breast-feed for much longer than was healthy for her or her baby. In the end, her son was diagnosed with failure to thrive at his one-month appointment—she wasn't producing enough milk, so he wasn't getting enough to eat—and as soon as she switched to formula, he immediately started gaining weight and thriving.

Anyway, all that said, here are some of the reasons that could mean that making the switch to formula is best for you and your baby.

1. **It just isn't working**. There are some moms who simply can't breast-feed. There are also some babies who simply can't breast-feed. Your nipples may be inverted. Your baby may be tongue-tied. You may not produce enough milk. Your baby may have an immature sucking reflex. Whatever the problem is, if it's not working, then stop. Your baby is much better off eating formula than struggling to get enough to eat.

2. **You adopted your baby**. My friend Janelle adopted a little girl last year and had nurse after lactation consultant after friend tell her that she should try to breast-feed. She tried medically induced lactation (it didn't work) and then tried buying milk from a milk bank. But when she realized that the milk bank was costing her more than her mortgage payment (milk banks can charge up to $4.50 per ounce), she switched to formula. And, oh my goodness, you should see her precious baby girl! She's perfect and beautiful and absolutely thriving.

3. **It's stressing you or your baby out**. My friend Megan was so stressed about breast-feeding her daughter that every time she got ready to feed, her shoulders got all tense, and in turn, her baby could sense her agitation and started to cry. This led to more frustration, more crying, and more failed feeding

sessions. If breast-feeding is getting too stressful, stop. Or take a break and let your baby have formula. A peaceful, comforting feeding with formula is hands-down better than a tear-filled, agitated breast-feeding session.

4. **It hasn't worked for you before**. I actually know several moms who had really stressful breast-feeding experiences with their first babies and started getting stressed about breast-feeding the instant they got pregnant for the second time. If you absolutely hated breast-feeding with your first baby, then I give you my official permission to skip the stress and start your second baby off on formula from day one. Stressing out about breast-feeding should not be your main concern when you're about to have a baby. (That said, my friend Sarah had a horrible experience breast-feeding her first baby and was shocked when her second baby latched on right away and had no problems at all, so struggling once doesn't necessarily mean you will every time.)

5. **You take a medication that is contraindicated with breast-feeding**. Almost everything you ingest—food, drinks, medications—will seep into your breast milk. Most of these things are completely harmless to your baby. But there are several medications that can harm your baby if he ingests them through your breast milk. If you take any medications on a regular basis—antidepressants, anti-inflammatory drugs, heart medications—call your doctor and find out if they are safe to use while breast-feeding.

6. **You have a medical reason**. Occasionally, there are situations where formula is the best medical choice for a baby. The most common one is failure to thrive—where a baby isn't getting enough milk to grow as he or she should when breast-feeding. Occasionally, babies can have a reaction to their mother's milk—often due to something the mom drinks or takes that precludes breast-feeding—that means it's better to feed them with formula.

Breast-Feeding: The First Two Weeks

When I was pregnant with Joey, my friend Stacy sat me down and told me she needed to have "the talk" with me. From there, she went on to tell me all of her been-there, done-that tricks and tips to being a successful breast-feeder. I took notes. And I referred back to those notes at least twenty-eight times in the first two weeks of my baby's life. Stacy's notes saved me when I was discouraged and ready to give up because my nipples were cracked and bleeding and it felt as though my son had razors in his mouth when he was sucking. And they encouraged me when I didn't think I could wake up even one more time at 2:00 a.m. to do a feeding.

I want to be your Stacy. I want to sit you down and talk you through those first tough weeks of breast-feeding. Because breast-feeding is hard. What seems like a simple point-and-shoot maneuver is actually really complicated and can cause a lot of pain, frustration, and tears (for both you and your baby). So, here are my been-there, done-that tips on how to survive your first two weeks of breast-feeding.

The Breast-Feeding Talk

1. **Make fourteen days your goal**. Repeat after me: fourteen days. Fourteen. That's ten plus four. Don't set your sights on exclusively breast-feeding for the next decade on day one. That's downright daunting. Instead, play a psychological mind game with yourself and make it your goal to breast-feed for the next fourteen days and after that you'll reassess. Then, when you're up in the middle of the night, rubbing Polysporin on your nipples, you can give yourself a pep talk to remind you the pain and frustration will be over soon.

2. **Remember: it will get easier**. Your nipples will heal. Your baby will figure out how to latch on. Your engorgement will decrease. You'll stop leaking all over your shirt. Wait; let me rephrase: you'll become an expert at remembering to wear breast pads so no one will notice when you leak all over your

shirt. And, at that point, you'll find that breast-feeding is—dare I say it?—actually enjoyable. You may actually start looking forward to breast-feeding sessions. And decide that you want to breast-feed for longer—maybe even much longer.

3. **Don't force it**. If you reach a moment when your baby is screaming and you're crying and no one seems able to latch on or stay latched, just pause for a few minutes. Hand your baby off to daddy, go check Facebook, and come back when you've calmed down to try again.

4. **Drink like a marathon runner**. To become a lean, mean, milk-producing machine, your body needs lots of fluids. So grab a glass of water and guzzle it before and after every feeding session to make sure you have the fluids you need.

5. **Eat well**. I started to write, "Eat like a sumo wrestler," but then I thought about the fact that devouring a carton of mint chip during a midnight feeding session is a little detrimental to the whole losing-the-baby-weight thing. So I'm changing my talk to say, "Eat well." While you're breast-feeding it's really important to make sure you're eating enough healthy, balanced meals and snacks to build your milk supply.

6. **Treasure this time**. There will be times (okay, lots of times) when your newborn feeds for an hour and a half only to take a twelve-minute break and want to feed again. You may start to feel like a human cow who lives and breathes to breast-feed your baby. But treasure it. Because your baby is going to grow. And those hourlong feeding sessions will fade into ten-minute power feeds. And then those power feeds will turn into, "Juice, mama!" and you'll look back on those marathon feeding sessions and get all weepy and emotional. And then people will stare at you as you sit at your computer in a coffee shop, with tears streaming down your face as you wax nostalgic about the good ole days when your baby snuggled in your lap and stared up at you with big, need-you eyes. (Not that I know about this from experience or anything.)

Breast-Feeding Gear

When I was at Buy Buy Baby, registering for my baby shower, I noticed there was a whole section on the registry "suggestion" list for breast-feeding gear. And, naive new mama that I was, I turned to the lady helping me with my registry and asked her why in the world you'd need gear for a simple open-mouth-insert-breast maneuver. She shook her head and plastered on one of those you'll-find-out-soon-enough smiles. And I did find out. Here's what you're going to need.

1. **A nursing pillow**. A nursing pillow is basically a moon-shaped pillow that supports your baby while she feeds so you can give your already-exhausted arms a rest. And in my opinion, this is undoubtedly the most important piece of nursing gear there is—yes, that's right; I'm ranking it higher than a nursing bra, only because it provides so much convenience and comfort. A good, supportive nursing pillow will not only save your back, but will also free up your arms to do important things, like hold a latte or read a book. I'm not super-opinionated about which type of pillow to buy. I used a Boppy for all three of my kids and really liked it, but I've also heard good things about My Breast Friend (ha!) pillows, which have the added bonus of a strap that allows you to nurse totally hands-free.

2. **A good nursing bra**. Let's just say that when your breasts double (okay, quadruple) in size overnight, they're going to need support. That paired with the reality that when your baby decides she's hungry, she's hungry, and the faster you can get yourself situated and ready to feed, the better. Forewarning: don't go out and buy seven new nursing bras before you have your baby. When I was in my nesting stage, I went to Special Addition and bought four (yes, four) nursing bras. I am normally a size D, and when I'm pregnant, that gets rounded up to a double D. Since I had been warned that my boobs were going to be ginormous, I bought quad Ds, joking

as I paid for them that I'd have to stuff them with breast pads to make them fit. But, three weeks later, when I exchanged said bras for size F (yes, they make that), I decided that from then on, all nursing bra purchases were relegated to post-baby shopping excursions.

3. **Sleep bras and nursing tanks**. Aside from a few regular nursing bras, you may also want to pick up a few sleep bras. These are soft, cotton bras that serve the sole purpose of supporting your breasts and holding breast pads in place when you sleep. You could, of course, use a normal nursing bra for this purpose, but sleep bras are super-comfortable and, well, if you're getting fewer than three hours of sleep at night, you may as well be comfortable while you do it. You may also want to pick up a nursing tank or two. They're great not only for lounging around the house, but also for wearing under your clothes when you do decide to venture out in public.

4. **A breast pump—maybe**. Let's do a little exercise together. Close your eyes and imagine yourself six months from now. Are you: (a) (still) camped out on your couch, wearing ratty sweats, with your legs propped up on your coffee table and a feeding baby in your lap; or are you (b) wearing a power suit and lugging a cooler full of bottles into your office at work while you try to find a private place to breast-feed?

If you picked the first choice, you may not need a breast pump at all. I'm a work-from-home mom, which means I work from my couch (yes, wearing ratty sweats) and have hardly ever had need for a breast pump. And on those rare occasions when my husband and I decide to do something crazy, like go out to dinner without the kids, I can easily get enough milk for one feeding using an inexpensive hand pump.

But if you picked choice B, you're going to need a pump—and a good one. If you plan on going back to work—even for a few hours a week—you're going to need to pump while at work in order to keep your milk supply up and produce enough milk for your baby to have while he's away from you. Trust me: you don't want to be stuck at work, hunched in a bathroom stall, using a hand pump for thirty minutes when you should be in a finance meeting. Splurge on a fast and efficient electric pump (my working-mom friend's recommendation is the Medela Pump In Style) and you'll make pumping at work a lot easier on yourself.

5. **A nursing cover**. My in-laws came to stay with me for a week after I had my son—which was a good thing—but it made it so every time I needed to feed the baby, I had to disappear upstairs into the nursery and shut the door for an hour while Joey ate. I learned really quickly that with the help of a nursing cover—and some strategic positioning—I could feed my baby and still be part of the action.

(Somewhat Productive) Things to Do While Breast-Feeding

I know that I told you when we had "the talk" that you need to treasure every moment when your baby is breast-feeding. And you should treasure each and every eighty-minute, never-ending feeding session. What a precious time to bond and get to know your baby! But—and I'm not ashamed to admit this—I could only gaze into my baby's eyes for so long before getting bored and sleepy. And when I was running on too-little sleep to begin with, there were times when I needed something to do while sitting in that rocker. Here are some ideas:

1. **Pray for your baby.** What a great opportunity nursing gives us to pray for our babies! As you sit there, it's a great chance to cry out to God in gratitude for the incredible blessing of your child—and pray for your baby's growth, development, future, and more.

2. **Read a novel.** I am a novel junkie. There is nothing better

than getting involved in a really great story. And being forced to sit down during a feeding session means more time to read. My recommendation is to pick up a Kindle or Nook to read on—not only are e-readers lightweight, but they allow you to turn pages with one hand when you have a nursing baby on your lap. Plus, there have been many times that my Kindle has saved me from a meltdown (me, not my baby) when I finish a book in the middle of a feeding session and can buy another novel with one click on Amazon.com.

3. **Read your Bible**. I always reserve the first morning nursing session for Bible reading, and it's a great way to ensure that I fit time for Jesus in my jam-packed day.

4. **Do a devotional**. You could also spend either your first or last nursing session of the day reading through a daily devotional. Once again, reading while you're nursing virtually guarantees that you won't miss a day (you're not going to forget to feed your baby, are you?) and can be very uplifting for your new-mama soul.

5. **Sing to your baby**. I have one of those voices that would get featured on the laugh track for *American Idol*—it's not pretty. But my babies seem to love it. So, while they're eating, I sing them my favorite hymns and songs.

6. **Work on your marriage**. Even though your baby has become the focus of most of your waking thoughts, your husband (remember him?) still needs you too. So ask him to join you in the nursery during a feeding session, and use the time to just talk to each other.

7. **Read magazines**. Having a new baby tends to fry your ability to have educated conversations—but pick up a couple of magazines and you'll have a whole list of potential conversation topics (read the table of contents) that will make it sound as though you're getting way more than two hours of sleep in a night.

8. **Catch up with friends**. Remember back in the day when you

could chat on the phone for hours and hours with your best girlfriend? Well, now you suddenly have time to do that again. Get your baby set nursing, put your earpiece in, and call up a long-lost friend.

9. **Plan your dinner menu...for Christmas.** Naturally, the last thing you're going to do for the next few months is cook. But that shouldn't stop you from dusting off your favorite cookbook and folding the pages of the recipes that you're going to make once you're out of the baby phase.

10. **Check Facebook, Pinterest, or Twitter.** This may be the one and only time in your life that someone calls checking Facebook productive, but hey, if you're just sitting there, there's no reason not to find out what your second-grade best friend is doing or scope out some crafts that you'll never actually do on Pinterest.

· ·

Time-Out for Mom

For When You're Treasuring a Quiet Moment with Your Baby

"This is what the LORD says—your Redeemer, who formed you in the womb: I am the LORD, the Maker of all things, who stretches out the heavens, who spreads out the earth by myself." (Isaiah 44:24)

Lord God, You are the Great Redeemer! I sit here in awe that You—the One who made the heavens and the earth, also carefully knit together this tiny, precious life that I now hold in my arms. Thank You, Father, for not only creating and loving my baby, but also for giving him the opportunity to be redeemed by grace. You are forever faithful. Amen.

· ·

Breast-Feeding in Public

Last summer I flew to Nashville to attend the MOPS convention, and since my son Will was only two months old, I brought him with me. The day before we left, my pediatrician warned me that he had some fluid in his ears (he was developing an ear infection) and that the best way to keep his ears from hurting on the plane was to feed him during both takeoff and landing. Easy enough, right?

But I was flying Southwest. And while most mothers of newborns who are traveling alone would think ahead enough to print out a boarding pass twenty-four hours in advance, I am not most moms. I forgot. So I ended up with the last middle seat on the plane between a 320-pound guy and a college-athlete type carrying a bagful of McDonald's burgers.

I'm sure you can imagine how well it went over when I slipped on my nursing cover and propped my elbow up on the armrest to breast-feed my son. My college friend pressed his call button and asked if he could have another seat (there wasn't one available), and my other friend glared at me while trying to avert his eyes. Needless to say, I couldn't get off that flight fast enough.

My point? There are going to be times you can't help but feed your baby in public. And while I'm not the kind of lactivist who participates in nurse-ins in Target (although if that's your thing, more power to you), I am the kind of lactivist who thinks it's entirely appropriate to feed your baby in public when necessary. Here are my tips for doing so gracefully.

1. **Bring a nursing cover everywhere you go**. A receiving blanket or your old college sweatshirt just isn't going to cut it—one quick move from your baby and the thing will fly off right as your old geometry teacher walks by. Instead, get in the habit of always carrying a nursing cover in your diaper bag so you can quickly cover up when you need to.

2. **Be confident**. If you are hiding in a corner, facing backward in the middle of a restaurant, you look pretty suspicious. I've

found that if I quietly and discreetly cover up and then continue on with whatever I'm doing, most people around me won't even notice what I'm doing.

3. **Wear clothes that lend themselves to breast-feeding**. I'll never forget the Sunday I wore my one-piece, zip-up-the-back dress to church. Let's just say that we had to leave church early that day.

4. **Ask for help**. It can be a bit tricky to get yourself all situated to feed—so don't be afraid to ask a friend to help you adjust your nursing cover or grab you a burp rag from your diaper bag.

(Sort-of) Private Places to Feed in Public

1. A store dressing room.
2. In your car.
3. In a department store lounge. Many department stores have women's lounges that double as quiet places to breast-feed.
4. On a bus or subway car—just sit in a corner and cover up.
5. In a restaurant booth. (Bonus: order yourself some iced tea and you'll get some R & R while your baby eats.)
6. At the park. Find a quiet bench or a patch of grass in the shade.
7. On the couch in a coffee shop.
8. Some baby-friendly stores (Babies "R" Us, for example) have nursing lounges that are all set up with comfy chairs and dim lights for breast-feeding moms.
9. In a book nook at the library or a bookstore.

Weaning

Confession: I don't like to wean my kids. I like breast-feeding, and the thought of giving up that special time of bonding and comfort makes me get all teary. So instead of weaning my kids at, say, one year of age, I just keep on breast-feeding them. And breast-feeding. And breast-feeding. I did eventually wean my daughter just before her second birthday—after my husband forced me to go on a trip with just him for our anniversary—but I cried for two days while freaking out that she was going to be scarred for life because I weaned her. Can you say, hormonal?

I hope I don't offend anyone by saying this, but I do think there comes a point in every baby's life when they need to wean. And that point is probably before they start kindergarten. If you Google "breast-feeding recommendations," you'll find that most pediatricians agree that breast-feeding for at least a year is ideal—and going beyond that to even two or three years can't hurt.

Of course, recommendations from the medical community have to be countered against practicality—and the truth is that it's really hard for a lot of women to continue breast-feeding for a full year, especially if they work. I polled my friends, and most of them weaned somewhere between six and nine months, with about a quarter of them making it to a full year and one or two of us going beyond that.

Regardless of when you wean, it has to be a process. I had to wean my son Joey cold turkey when he was sixteen months old because I got pregnant and had to go on a drug that was contraindicated with breast-feeding. I literally went from feeding him four times a day to nothing overnight. And let me just say that it was painful. Worse than the engorgement I felt when I started breast-feeding. So don't do that unless you absolutely have to.

The best way to wean is to slowly remove one feeding every day over the course of a few weeks. Once you're down to one feeding a day, start doing that only every other day, and eventually, just stop feeding. If you feel any engorgement, you can use cabbage leaves or bind your breasts with a tight sports bra or an ACE bandage. Whatever you do, don't pump when you're engorged unless you absolutely have to, because that would—you guessed it—cause your body to produce more milk.

Breast-Feeding FAQs

Question: Can I (pretty pretty please, because I really don't think I'll survive the next two hours without a latte) drink coffee while breast-feeding?

Answer: As a general rule, caffeine is just fine while breast-feeding. And now that I'm your best friend forever for giving you back your double non-fat mochas with whip, I want to caution you that drinking large amounts of caffeine (say, three to four cups in a day) can make your baby jittery and cause sleep disturbances. (That goes for both you and Junior, by the way.) Likewise, some babies have systems that struggle to deal with caffeine. My son Joey was getting really gassy and fussy after every breast-feeding session, and I finally figured out after two weeks of denial that my coffee habit was affecting his system. I switched to chai tea, and his fussiness all but disappeared. A few months later, after his digestive system had matured a bit, I was able to reintroduce coffee slowly, and he did just fine.

Question: Can I drink alcohol while breast-feeding?

Answer: Maybe. Before ordering that margarita, I suggest you talk to your OB, midwife, lactation consultant, or pediatrician and get some guidelines. That said, my OB told me that alcohol is typically absorbed into the breast milk fairly quickly (the spike is about thirty to forty-five minutes after drinking) and disappears just as quickly, so she recommended that I wait approximately two hours after having a drink to breast-feed, just to be supersafe. Also, since drinking large quantities of alcohol can be detrimental both to your breast-feeding ability and your overall health, it's probably best to limit your alcohol intake to one small drink, max, at any given time.

Question: If I do drink, can't I just pump and dump?

Answer: For years, women have been told that if they have a few glasses of wine while breast-feeding, they can just pump, toss the milk away, and then feed their babies normally. And this would make sense if your breasts were like pitchers that got filled and emptied and then refilled again. But reality is that your body is a complex, moving system that is constantly making breast milk, reabsorbing what isn't used, and replenishing its supply lines. That said, if there is alcohol in your bloodstream, there is alcohol in your breast milk, which means pumping and dumping is futile. So your best bet is to limit yourself to one or two drinks max and to wait at least two hours for the alcohol to clear from your bloodstream before feeding your baby.

Question: What about food? Are there any foods that are off-limits while breast-feeding?

Answer: Kinda sorta. How's that for a definitive answer? Here's the deal: Unlike pregnancy, there are no "unsafe" foods for nursing moms. So you can go ahead and eat turkey sandwiches and sushi to your heart's content. But certain foods (like that super-spicy curry that you pick up at the Garage-majal) can change the flavor of your breast milk, meaning your baby will be less likely to happily eat it. Additionally, some foods can make some babies gassy, fussy, or irritable, meaning that if you're dealing with a colicky or fussy baby, your first line of defense may be to consider removing common irritants like dairy, wheat, or soy from your diet.

Question: I'm a bridesmaid in my cousin's wedding, and I'll be away from my baby all day. I have plenty of breast milk in the freezer for her to eat that day, so can I just skip the pumping and resume breast-feeding as normal the next day?

Answer: That depends on how well established breast-feeding is for you. If your baby is teeny-tiny and is still getting into a breast-feeding routine, you'll probably need to pump at normal feeding times to make sure (a) your milk supply doesn't diminish, and (b) you don't leak breast milk all over that $250 silk bridesmaid dress. If you've been breast-feeding for a while, you may be able to make it for longer, although even then it can be risky. Case in point: me. I work from home, so I've never been away from my baby for more than a few hours. But a few weeks ago, my company flew my team into town for a retreat, and I had to work a regular eight-to-five workday at the office. I figured that skipping on pumping for a day would be just fine since not only is my son twelve months old, but I've also breast-fed for more than four and a half years of my life at this point, between my three kids. But even with a well-established breast-feeding career, by mid-afternoon I was not only engorged but also stuffing toilet paper into my bra to keep from leaking all over my work shirt.

Beyond Breast-Feeding

See, I told you breast-feeding was complicated. And while you probably feel that I just loaded you up with information, there's still a lot more you need to know about feeding your baby that goes beyond basic breast-feeding. In the next chapter, I'm going to fill you in on pumping, milk storage, bottle-feeding, formula feeding, feeding schedules, and more. So go grab yourself a glass of water—remember: nursing mothers need to stay hydrated—and a healthy-ish snack and come right back.

SIX

To the Bottle and Beyond

The Nitty (and Hopefully Not Gritty) Details You Need to Bottle-Feed

've made lots of mistakes as a mom. There was the time I forgot to buy diapers and ended up wrapping Kate in a towel so I could go to the store to buy Huggies. And the time I had to feed my Joey dry Cheerios for breakfast before school because I was out of milk, bread, and eggs. And I don't even want to talk about the time I forgot Will in the church nursery and was five minutes down the road before I realized I was heading home sans baby.

But the mistake I probably regret more than any other (to this point) is choosing not to introduce my babies to bottle-feeding when they were young enough to adapt. And the worst part? I made the same mistake three times. With three different babies. Can you say *slow learner*?

It all started with Joey. Doctors and nurses warned me not to introduce the bottle until I knew breast-feeding was well established. Someone threw out the term "nipple confusion," and I shuddered. I did not want my son to get confused or do something crazy, like enjoy using a bottle when he could be breast-feeding. So I waited the obligatory two to three weeks to make sure nursing was well established and then tacked on an extra couple of weeks just to be on the safe side. Bad move. By the time I introduced Joey to the bottle, he wanted absolutely nothing to do with it. Which was fine when I was at home. But when he was four months old and I got the opportunity to go to New York for a work trip and he refused to take a bottle from my mom (who came along and stayed in the hotel room to take care of him), I was in trouble. They actually had to call me out of my work meetings to breast-feed.

You would think that after that experience, I would've been on top of introducing Kate to the bottle. But no. Instead, with her, I got really overwhelmed as I tried to juggle being the mom of two kids under two and completely forgot about introducing her to the bottle until she was four months old. And at that point, it was too late. Again.

With two strikes against me, I really had every incentive to make sure Will was a bottle-feeding champ. I mean, after all, I had lots of experience with bottle-feeding failure and you'd think I would've been motivated by, say, the opportunity to have someone else get up in the middle of the night to feed him every once in a while. And I was motivated. Just not motivated enough to fight through the whining and protesting he did. To my defense, Will did eventually take a bottle when he was five months old. One time— and out of desperation because I was gone and daddy didn't have the equipment to feed him any other way.

All that said, I want to repeat what I said in the last chapter, that there is absolutely nothing wrong with giving your baby a bottle from time to time. Or every day. In fact, it may be just the thing you need to survive your first few months as a mom. It also may come in handy if you, say, want to go back to work or go on a date with your husband, and you need to have a something other than your boobs with which to nourish your baby.

So now that I've sufficiently established that I am absolutely unqualified to talk to you about bottle-feeding in every way, I'm going to go ahead and spend the rest of the chapter telling you how to do things that I have no idea how to do. But don't worry. I asked my bottle-feeding friends to help me out. Here's all of their advice.

Bottle Basics

I actually blame Target for my bottle-using failure. Because if the bottle aisle wasn't so completely overwhelming, I would've maybe felt more inclined to at least consider buying a bottle. Maybe. But seriously, what are there—like, a gazillion choices? And even once you hone in on a brand, you have to decide on nipple size and bottle size and bottle-cover color, and within a few minutes you find yourself having to take a cool-down break in the in-store Starbucks before you start to hyperventilate.

When you recover from your panic, my friend Alex suggests that you start with the cheapest bottles—provided they are BPA-free—and see if your baby seems to like them. If he does, then you're all set. If your baby gets fussy, colicky, or gassy when using your cheap bottles, then you should probably start teaching him some lessons about entitlement. I mean, does he really think he can just have everything handed to him through a silver-plated nipple?

Naturally, if you're one of those enlightened parents who decides to wait until your baby can understand what you're saying before teaching him character lessons, you could also head back to the store and see if you can find a bottle that will meet your baby's unique needs and preferences. My sister, Alisa, loves Born Free bottles because they don't leak and are great for reducing gas, and she likes that there's a glass bottle option. My friend Anna uses Dr. Brown's bottles because they're made especially to help colicky babies, and she's found they really help to reduce gas. And my friend Candace loves using Playtex Drop-Ins because they have disposable liners that make cleanup a breeze. There's even fancy breast-simulating bottles that have these nipples that mimic a breast and help babies who go back and forth between the breast and bottle. And get this: with some of these breast-to-bottle bottles, you can even get an adapter kit for your breast pump to pump straight into them. Talk about the Cadillac of all Cadillacs.

Anyway, once you've decided on a bottle brand, the hard part is over. From there, you can just follow the age guidelines on the box to figure out nipple size. As far as bottle size, you can just go ahead and assume your baby is going to drink a lot and get the super-big gulp size. Or whatever looks right.

Pumping

Reason #1405 that I never bottle-fed: I hate pumping. For some reason the idea of sitting with valves and pulleys and throbbing tubes stuck to my boobs doesn't appeal to me. At all. But as horrible as it is, there are lots of moms out there who do it and do it diligently. My sister-in-law Annie pumped several times a day for an entire year, all while trying to juggle being a working mom. Talk about dedication.

If you're going to pump a lot (like if you're going back to work), you'll want to invest in an electric double-breast pump. Trust me: hiding out in a bathroom stall while using a hand pump is not a good idea—as nice as it sounds to have built-in breaks in your workday. And as I said in the last chapter, if you just plan on pumping occasionally, a much less expensive hand pump will do.

You may also want to consider investing in a hands-free pumping bra. As if sitting alone in a room, hooked up to a machine that's milking you, isn't enough, breast pumps require you to hold them up to each boob the entire time you're pumping. Which means you can't do anything productive, like check your e-mail or even read your Kindle while pumping. A pumping bra will hold the breast shields onto your breasts for you—which is very disturbing to look at but quite handy when it comes to multitasking.

Now, for some basic medical rules that I read online and confirmed with my friend who is a lactation consultant (you're welcome!): Every time you pump, you want to make sure you empty your breasts—which takes about ten to fifteen minutes using a good, strong electric pump. An empty breast signals your body to make more milk, while a half-emptied breast tells your body to make less. Frequent, short pumping sessions could cause your milk supply to go down. If you're pumping after your baby nurses, then you can just pump until you notice that nothing is coming out.

Breast Milk Storage Rules

As if keeping track of your baby's diaper habits and feeding schedule (using an iPad and an app, of course) weren't enough for you to do, you also need to learn some important safety rules about the storage of breast milk. Because, well, if you don't follow the rules, your baby will get sick. And it will be all your fault. Not to put any pressure on you or anything. Here's what you'll need to do:

- Fresh milk can be left at room temperature if it will be used within six hours. But don't refrigerate fresh milk after it's been sitting out for more than an hour.
- If you are planning on storing the milk, refrigerate or freeze it immediately.
- Store your milk in small portions so you don't waste it if your baby can't finish it. You worked hard for that milk, after all.
- Fresh milk can be stored five days in the fridge and three to six months in a freezer. If you want to store it longer, it will last six to twelve months in a deep freeze.
- Write the date you pumped on the milk storage bag in Sharpie. This is the perfect excuse to go buy the jumbo-

sized rainbow pack of Sharpies you've been wanting. And try to use the milk in the order you pumped it.

- ∽ Thaw frozen milk in the refrigerator or in cold water, not on the counter.
- ∽ After you thaw frozen milk, you can keep it in the fridge for up to twenty-four hours, but don't refreeze it.
- ∽ Never use a microwave to thaw or warm breast milk. It could create hot pockets that could burn your baby's mouth.
- ∽ Any milk that your baby doesn't drink from a bottle should be thrown out.
- ∽ If your baby prefers warm milk, place the bottle in a bowl of hot water and warm it up for ten minutes.

Formula Basics

I took a field trip to the formula aisle at the grocery store when I started writing this section and realized there is more than one kind of formula. I'm pretty sure I saw chocolate, strawberry, vanilla, and even butterscotch ripple. I didn't look very closely—but I swear, there were, like, a billion choices. Anyway, since I felt overwhelmed, I asked my friend Anna to help me sort them out.

Basically, most babies start off on a standard cow's milk formula. These are the "vanilla formulas"—the basic, standard powders that hospitals use and parents buy and pediatricians recommend. And unless your baby is allergic to cow's milk, you'll probably be really happy using a cow's milk formula until your baby graduates to actual cow's milk. If your baby does show signs of an allergy—bloody stool, gassiness, eczema—your pediatrician will switch you to a soy milk formula. If your baby still has an allergy after trying soy milk formula, then you'll be switched to a super-fancy butterscotch-ripple of a formula called protein hydrolysate formula. I have no idea what protein hydrolysate is, but I figure if your doctor has gone out of her way to recommend something that she can't even pronounce, then she has probably done her research. And you should probably just do what she says.

As far as buying formula, word on the street is that it's pretty darn expensive. Like more-than-your-latte-habit expensive. Anna tells me that club stores, like Costco and Sam's, are your best bet—but she warns that formula can expire pretty quickly, so check the poll date before buying a jumbo-sized barrel of the stuff. Also, there are lots of ready-mixed formulas on the market, which are super convenient but also super expensive. So if you have money to spare, feel free to spend your hard-earned money paying someone else to mix your formula for you. Or spend the twelve seconds it takes to mix it yourself. Up to you.

Preparing and Storing Formula

Formula is a lot like leftovers. Okay, formula is nothing like leftovers, except for the fact that it is usually best when mixed and eaten right away. You can store it in the refrigerator for up to twenty-four hours, but it won't taste as good. Or so I've heard.

If you're heading out, your best solution is to premeasure your dry formula powder into a small Tupperware container (or, if you have one, a fancy formula container) and pack it with you, along with several bottles of premeasured water. If that feels too complicated, you could also prep it before you leave and keep it cool in a cooler until you need it.

Of course, even after you figure out how to store and pack and mix your formula, your baby may throw a wrench at you. Get this: some babies like their milk warmed. You can buy a bottle warmer to warm it quickly or just put the bottle in a bowl of water. However, Anna recommends seeing if your baby will take a bottle at room temperature first. This will save you from having to heat it up in the middle of the night or find a way to warm your bottle on the go.

One last thing about mixing formula: the tap water in some cities isn't fit for infant consumption. There are lots of reasons for this—it could be higher in fluoride than is best for your baby, or it could have unhealthy levels of other minerals. Your safest bet is to mix your baby's formula with nursery water—which you can pick up supercheap (well, supercheap in comparison to formula) at the grocery store.

Feeding Adopted Babies

I actually know two women who were able to medically induce breast-feeding so they could feed their adopted infants—which has to be one of the coolest developments in modern medicine. I love that. But while some women are able to stimulate breast-feeding, the vast majority of adopted babies are bottle-fed. And while formula is the obvious and simplest choice, there are some adoptive moms who decide to pursue other options for various reasons.

My nephew Asa was adopted, and due to a serious medical condition, his doctors felt that breast milk was the best bet for his fragile digestive system. Luckily, there is a nonprofit milk bank in our area that takes donated breast milk and pasteurizes it for at-risk infants and preemies. My nephew was able to get a prescription for breast milk, and while it was very expensive—almost five dollars an ounce— it was a huge blessing for little Asa when he didn't have another option.

I've also heard that some adoptive parents choose to go a kind of modern-day wet nurse route where they use other people's milk to feed their baby. They basically ask their nursing friends and relatives to pump for their baby or talk to moms who are weaning and find out if they can take their frozen breast milk stash. I've even heard stories of moms buying breast milk on Craigslist.com! If you want to go this route—and I can see how the benefits could outweigh the risk for some families—do it very cautiously. Breast milk is a body fluid, and certain diseases can pass into the breast milk, so make sure to talk to your pediatrician, and most important, make sure you know the person pumping for you on a personal level. And no, "We met on Craigslist" does not count as personal.

It's a Brave New World, Isn't It?

Just to close out this chapter on a high note, I figured this would be a good time to remind you how much you've changed since becoming a mom. Because if you had said any of these things ten months ago, your friends would've thought you were crazy. But now? Just part of the everyday conversation.

10 Things You Never Would've Said Ten Months Ago . . . (But Are Totally Appropriate Now)

1. "Hey, can you run and get me a bottle of boob juice out of the fridge?"
2. "No, honey, I think these nipples look more like mine. Don't you think? I know those say that they are the most human-like nipples on the market, but I'm just not buying it."
3. "Do you think my breast pump counts as a carry-on item or a personal item?"
4. "No, you may not use the baby's milk in your cereal. Go to the store and get your own."
5. "Does this pumping bra make me look like Madonna? Wait. Don't answer that."
6. "I don't see why we can't use the bottles as dinner glasses. At least it'll buy me another day before I have to do the dishes."
7. "His poop does look a tiny bit greener on that new formula. Maybe we should go get some paint samples so we can accurately chart the color changes for the pediatrician."
8. "Honey, I know it's 3:00 a.m., but could you go to the store? We're out of (nursery) water."
9. "Don't you dare throw those last two drops down the drain. This is liquid gold, I'm telling you, liquid gold."
10. "Sorry, I can't help you weed the garden. I have to go pump."

SEVEN

Diapers and Wipers

Diapering Your Baby Like a Pro

iapering seems like such a simple concept. A diaper here, a wipe there, a clean, dry, and happy baby in your arms that has absolutely no chance of peeing all over your brand-new suede coat. But like everything that has to do with kids, there's always an X factor—one little thing that steps in and makes even the simplest things much more difficult. And, in this case, the X factor happens to be the fact that no matter how much you'd like to spreadsheet your baby's excretory habits (or is that just me?), you're never going to be able to predict when and how much your baby is going to poop or pee. Which means every mom out there is going to have a story to tell about a diapering fail.

Of course, new moms listen to these stories with relish. In fact, just to get you started, here are a few of the best ones I've heard lately:

- A few weeks ago, my friend Ashley found herself without a spare diaper at her friend's rehearsal dinner and ended up stuffing her son's pants with paper towels in the ladies' room while she sent her husband to the mini-mart for a pack of Huggies.
- My friend Laura's daughter had a blowout so extreme that it leaked through her car seat *and* the car seat base onto the car's actual seat. And, naturally, her husband borrowed her car the next day to pick up some coworkers from the airport and found a nasty surprise when he went to move the seat to make room for his guests.
- Perhaps my favorite story came from my friend Katie, who was holding her son while at a baby shower. The hostess announced that Katie had won a game, and she stood up to accept her prize and looked down to see poop from a diaper blowout running down her leg and onto the floor. Ew.

I love these stories. I laugh. I cry. And then I spend the next ten minutes reliving each story in my mind while feeling immensely grateful that I'm not the only mom in the world who can't seem to remember to pack a sufficient supply of diapers when I leave the house.

Anyway, all this is to say that even if you feel you're an utter failure at diapering, you're not. Everyone has those stories to share. And as you deal with that one cringe-worthy moment, when you're walking through the mall with a baby who is literally dripping out of his socks, you can rest assured that you'll think it's funny in a few years. At least a little funny.

In the meantime, I've put together this handy guide to help you get through diapering and wipering your child with finesse—well, as much finesse as a mom who is dealing with poop and pee can have. So here are my tips on how to choose diapers, how to use diapers, how to buy diapers, and how to make sure you choose, use, and buy diapers in the right order at the right time.

Time-Out for Mom

For When You're Doing the Mundane

"Trust in the Lord with all your heart and lean not on your own understanding; in all your ways submit to him, and he will make your paths straight." (Proverbs 3:5–6)

Father God, there are days where all I do is change diapers and rock this baby to sleep. But I pray that You will use me for your kingdom even in those small tasks. Help me follow You joyfully and fully so my baby will see Your love through me even in the first months of his life. Amen.

· ·

Choosing the Right Diapers

Just to make sure you get all the information you need to properly wipe and dipe your baby, I did a little research. In my well-equipped (read: I have a baby that needs diapers), home-based lab, I tested the various kinds of diapers so I'd be able to give you the authoritative scoop on the exact diapers to buy and use for your baby. My conclusion? They're all the right choice . . . sometimes.

The truth is that there are definite pros and cons to all types of diapers. So while one diaper type really outshines the others in efficiency, it may lag behind in convenience and cost. So, in an effort to bring my readers the best and most updated research. I sent this list out to a group of researchers (ie, my very helpful mommy girlfriends) to see what they had to say about each of these types. So there you have it: the first ever authoritative(-ish) study on diapers.

1. Brand-Name Disposable Diapers:

The Scoop: When I asked my panelists what types of diapers they used, the vast majority said either Huggies or Pampers.

Pros:

- Disposables are nothing if they're not convenient—you just wrap, toss, and go.
- If you run out of diapers in the middle of the night, you don't have to drive twenty-eight miles to find a store that carries them. Pretty much any mini-mart or drugstore will have them in stock.

Cons:

- Diapers definitely aren't cheap, especially when you throw in the extra buck you pay as a premium to buy the name brands.
- There is a level of environmental guilt—disposables can take up to five hundred years in a landfill to biodegrade—so throwing away hundreds of diapers a month definitely makes you wish there were a more eco-friendly alternative.

2. Generic Disposable Diapers

The Scoop: The "Wal-pers" and "Targgies" of the world—store-brand diapers that are created directly by manufacturers to mimic the name brands.

Pros:

- Just like brand-name disposable diapers, generic diapers are convenient and easy to use.
- Generics are readily available. You're not going to have to search high and low to find a pack.
- You get all the convenience of a disposable diaper at a much lower cost. Win-win.

Cons:

- Generics are unpredictable. Some of my panelists found a brand they loved and stuck to it. Others said that every time they decide to try generic, they regret it because the number of accidents immediately triples.
- Generics are just as bad for the environment as disposables.

3. Fancy Cloth Diapers

The Scoop: These adorable (try looking on Etsy.com!) diapers are made from a double layer of absorbent fabric and use either Velcro or snaps for fastening. Then, typically, a small cotton insert is added to the diaper for extra protection.

Pros:

- Talk about adorable—you'll hardly want to get your baby dressed because she looks so darn cute in her diapers.
- Cloth diapers are significantly better for the environment than disposables. Yes, there is the issue that you'll use a lot more water to wash them, but in comparison, cloth diapers win, hands-down.
- If you wash cloth diapers yourself, they're very inexpensive. Once you've paid the initial cost of buying your diapers, your costs are minimal.
- There is some research out there that shows cloth diapers are better for a baby's skin, although this hasn't been studied in depth and the results of my personal study indicate that diaper rash and skin issues are more linked to the individual baby than the type of diaper.

Cons:

- Cloth diapers tend to leak a bit more than disposables.
- If you hire a diaper service to pick up and wash your diapers, it can be fairly expensive. On the flip side, if you don't hire a diaper service, you'll end up spending quite a bit of time washing your baby's diapers.

- The initial cost to buy your cloth diapers and diaper covers can be quite expensive.

4. Generic Cloth Diapers

The Scoop: By far the cheapest way to diaper, absorbent white cotton square diapers are secured by pins or a fancy snap fastener. Then, generally, a plastic pair of protective pants are worn over the diaper to help protect from leaks.

Pros:
- Cloth diapers are really inexpensive. You'll have the initial cost of buying diapers and covers and snaps, but after that, the only thing you're paying for is some extra detergent. Even if you hire a diaper service to wash your diapers for you, you'll still probably spend less than you would on disposables.
- Better for the environment—you'll throw away about one-tenth the amount of waste that you would with disposables.

Cons:
- Cloth diapers tend to leak. A lot. So if you go this route, make sure to buy plenty of plastic diaper covers and carry a change of clothes.
- It can be a real pain to scrub poo off of diapers before you load them in the wash and to make sure you always have a fresh supply.

5. G-Diapers

The Scoop: G-Diapers are a cloth/disposable hybrid that start with a cute, washable fabric cover. Then you snap a plastic liner inside the cover and add a flushable, disposable, biodegradable insert into the plastic liner to create a diaper that's both disposable and washable.

Pros:
- This is the only diaper solution that's virtually guilt-free

when it comes to the environment. The cloth covers can be worn several times (minimizing laundry), and the inserts are flushable and biodegradable.

- G-diapers work really well. I actually used them with my daughter and found that when it came to effectiveness, G-diapers work just as well as brand-name disposables.
- G-diapers are supercute—they come in adorable colors, and it's about the cutest thing ever to see your baby's little patooty covered in a G.

Cons:

- The flushing process is a bit complicated. It uses a swish stick, and there are times that you just don't have time to deal with it.
- G-diapers are expensive. The cloth covers pose an expensive up-front cost, and then the liners are about the prices of brand-name diapers on their own.
- When there is a leak or accident, you end up having to clean up both the plastic liner (I washed them in the sink) and the cloth cover (in the washing machine).

Diaper Rash

For some reason, I had always believed that babies only get diaper rash when their parents aren't diapering and wipering them well. So when I noticed that my two-week-old baby Will had diaper rash so badly that it was bleeding, the first thing I did was call the nurse's line at my pediatrician's office and blurt out that "I gave my son diaper rash!" as if it were akin to child abuse. The nurse reassured me that my son's diaper rash was probably not my fault at all and that with a few simple steps, I could clear it right up. (Whew. Cross that off my list of ways I could possibly damage my kids for life.) Here's what you can do to avoid and treat diaper rash:

- Change your baby's diaper as soon as possible when you notice it's wet or dirty.
- If you're seeing a flat, bright-red rash on your baby's little bottom, smother it with a store-bought diaper rash cream. Zinc oxide–based creams, like Desitin or Balmex, work great. If you want to go the all-natural route, try Aveeno cream or Boudreaux's Butt Paste.
- If your baby has a bumpy red rash that looks like raw hamburger, it's probably a fungal infection, and the normal diaper creams mentioned above won't work. Try Lotrimin AF cream—yep, the stuff you use for athlete's foot—or call your doctor for a prescription.
- Let your baby's little bottom dry out bare buck for as long as you dare before putting on a new diaper.
- Soak your baby's tender areas in a warm bath, and use mild soap whenever you can.
- If you notice bleeding, cracking, or if it's so painful that your baby can't sleep, call your doctor.

Choosing the Right Wipes

Wipes are a bit easier to choose than diapers—mostly because, aside from fancy scents and added lotions and potions, most wipes are the same. A wipe is a wipe is a wipe. And that means that unless your baby has super-sensitive skin—or you have an affinity for lavender-scented things—you can probably just buy whichever wipes are cheapest. That said, I do have a few wiper-choosing tips:

- **Buy in bulk**. A refill pack costs about half as much per wipe as the ones that come in those handy plastic tubs. So buy in bulk and refill for the best of both worlds.
- **Buy lots**. The last thing you want to do is run out of wipes at an inconvenient time. I'll just allow you to let that sink in

for a little bit and I bet you'll be nice and motivated to head to Target and stock up. It can't ever hurt to have an extra package of wipes hanging around.

- **Don't put a limit on wipe use.** I have a friend whose husband—a frugal guy—limits her to two wipes per diaper change. Not only is this semi-ridiculous because wipes cost something like a half a cent each (I didn't do any math so I might be wrong on that), but also it's probably better to be thorough with the wipes than to save a few pennies and walk around with a baby who smells like poop all day. I figure that even the most liberal wipe users in the world will spend a grand total of about twenty-six dollars more per year than a wipe skimper (okay, so I didn't do any math here, either, but you get the point). Money well spent, in my opinion.

Saving Money on Diapers and Wipers

Now that I've effectively ranted about the evils of wipe-skimping, I feel I need to clear my name in frugal-mom circles by giving you some easy ways to save money on diapers and wipers. Plus, I figure if I save you some money here, it will quickly make amends for all the money you'll lose from upping your wipe limit to three or more wipes per diaper change. Anyway, as you already know, diapers and wipes are expensive—and to help you cut costs so you have enough money in the budget to satisfy your chocolate habit, here are some easy ways to save:

1. **Amazon Subscribe and Save**. If you sign up for Amazon Mom on Amazon.com, you can subscribe to an auto shipment of diapers and wipes. For example, I have them ship me a jumbo pack of Huggies and a refill pack of wipes every month. Not only do I save about 20 percent off what I'd pay at Target, but I also get them delivered to my doorstep so I don't have to worry about going to the store.

2. **Check couponing sites**. When I look in the newspaper or online, I often come up dry—ha!—when it comes to diaper coupons. I asked my friend Shellie, who runs the hugely popular couponing website savingwithshellie.com, and she said that diaper companies rarely run deals (I think they know they have an in-demand product) but that coupons do pop up from time to time. You just have to know where to look. Of course, the way I look at it is that if Shellie knows where to look (which she does), *and* she's going to post the deals she finds on her site, then I can skip the whole step of learning how to coupon and just nab coupons and deals from her.

3. **Sign up for store e-mails**. I get my best diapering deals from store e-mails. Just last week Babies "R" Us offered a free wipes refill pack with the purchase of any jumbo-sized package of Huggies. A few months ago, I scored a free ten-dollar gift card at Target for buying two boxes of diapers.

Three Basic Rules for Effective Diapering

1. Find diapers that fit. Diaper sizing is tricky. It doesn't seem as though it would be at first glance—one would think you could simply look at the weight range on the front of the diaper package and choose the appropriate diapers for your child's size. But assumptions like that are what leave you standing in the back of the church service, covered in pee (or worse), with a naked baby in your arms.

The truth is that every brand has a different "sizing profile," which means that while Huggies may fit perfectly around your baby's fat legs, Pampers may gap at just the wrong spot and leave you with an excessive amount of accidents. Or vice versa. My advice is to buy a few small packs of a few types and see which ones fit your baby well before buying a jumbo pack. Once you've found your brand, stick with it. There's no use risking your beautiful white carpet only to find out that the newest SuperDiapers just don't work as well as your tried-and-true favorites.

2. Stock up before starting a change. Just last week, my one-year-old (my *third* baby, I might add) needed a diaper change, and I got him to the table and took his diaper off and threw it away before realizing that I was (a) out of wipes, and (b) the only backup wipes were downstairs in the laundry room.

I picked up my baby and held him with both hands stuck straight out in front of me while I ran downstairs. All went well until the trip back up, when Will decided it was a perfect time to pee. You know; since he was hanging out there all easy breezy and all. And since I was running and screaming and flailing as he peed, the pee didn't land in one concise little puddle on the floor, but instead sprayed all over me, the wall, the carpet, and his shirt. Good times.

My point? You can avoid all this by simply doing two things: (1) keeping your diaper table area, as well as any other areas in your house where you may change diapers, fully stocked with all your diapering essentials—diapers, wipes, diaper cream—and (2) always checking to make sure you're not out of any essentials before you take the baby's diaper off.

3. Be prepared. The ability to keep your diaper arsenal fully stocked at all times and ready for any and every emergency is a skill only the most advanced newborn mamas can master (see "Diapering 201" on page 106). Trust me. Even I haven't quite figured that one out yet. But complicated as it is, I'll try to put it in layman's terms so you can at least begin to grasp what you're up against:

Step 1: Open your diaper bag.

Step 2: Put several diapers, a container of wipes, a changing pad, some diaper cream, and a change of clothes or two in said bag.

Step 3: Put said bag in the back of the car or in the stroller or over your shoulder so it can go with you to wherever you're going.

Three simple steps that have brought many a power mom to her knees. Three simple steps that have resulted in hundreds of tears of frustration and hours of Oxi-Cleaning. Three simple steps. My advice: Practice them, my friends. Practice them daily. Pack, repack, and pack again. And one day, you may be one of those people who is never caught in public without everything you need to diaper your baby. Good luck.

A Mastery of the Art of Diapering

Diapering and wipering isn't the most glamorous job—but someone has to do it, and that someone happens to be you. And now, as I leave this chapter, I want to leave you with an inspirational message—a message that I hope motivates you to dig in and be the best diaper-changing, wipe-lugging mom you can be. You master this, and your baby will be not only clean but confident—confident that you have wiped him and diped him to the best of your ability and are now sending him off onto the playground sparkling clean and ready to play. And to play with the clean kids.

And just to give you something to aspire to, I am going to conclude this chapter with five advanced diapering moves—moves that with practice and that Christian mom finesse that you're learning to embrace, you also can master. You can do this, oh hero of the Huggies and conquerer of the diaper champ. You can do this.

Diapering 201: Advanced Diapering Moves
for Moms Who Want to Be the Best
1. **Sanitizer Samba**. Managing to make the process of rubbing on hand sanitizer after a diaper change look like a little cha-cha-cha dance that never fails to make your baby smile.
2. **Fat-Roll Foresight**. A knack for knowing your kid is going to outgrow a diaper size before you buy the jumbo pack at Costco.

3. **Multi-Station Prep**. The art of keeping a completely stocked diapering station—a cute decorative basket complete with a changing pad and an ample supply of diapers, wipes, and butt cream—in convenient places around your house and car so you never have to go far to change a diaper.

4. **Speed Wrapping**. The ability to cover a surprise stream of pee—usually from a male baby—with a fresh diaper before the pee can get all over your shirt.

EIGHT

Gearing Up

Everything You Need (and Some Stuff You Don't) for Baby

n my pregnancy book, I told you that babies really only need four things: diapers/wipes, a car seat, somewhere to sleep, and something to wear. And while your mother-in-law is still probably trying to convince you that I am wrong and that babies do, in fact, need teeny-tiny hee-larious hot-pink high heels (yes, they make those), I still hold to my original assertion: your baby does not need most of the things the baby stores say he does.

I am, however, willing to admit that there is a very fine line between "need" and "my life would be a whole lot easier if I had this." At one point or another in my baby-raising career, I have bought, borrowed, or finagled nearly everything I could possibly put in that second make-my-life-easier category. Because you know what? I like convenience. And if something is going to make my life easier, I'm going to find a way to convince my husband that I need it. Even if I don't.

So, to recap, my totally confusing opinion on baby gear is that while you may only need four things to survive the first year of motherhood, there are a whole lot of things that will make your first year with your baby a lot easier. And because those things make your life easier and the last thing you need is to be stressed-out when you have a brand-new baby, those things you don't really need suddenly become things you probably do need. Make sense? I thought so.

To get you through this chapter quickly so you can get to the mall, I put together a list of my top baby gear "essentials" (yes, I had to put *essentials* in quotes due to my four-things theory) for each of your baby's first-year ages and stages. This is by no means a comprehensive list—you are going to need more things for your baby regardless of what people like me say—but it will at least get you started on the must-haves. For the rest, well, you can always count on your baby-high-heel-touting mother-in-law to give you a totally unbiased opinion.

Erin's Top Baby Gear Picks for Your Baby's First Year of Life

Baby Gear "Essentials" for Newborns

1. **A swaddling wrap**. You would think that after being scrunched up in a tiny space for nine months, your baby would want to sprawl out and stretch his legs. But no. Most newborns are comforted by being snuggled up tight, as they were in mommy's uterus, and the best way to replicate that feeling is by wrapping your little bundle up supertight in a swaddling wrap.

2. **A swing**. There's a reason that rock-a-bye-baby is the standard route to help calm a baby to sleep—it works. And while I know you love holding and rocking your little schnookums as much as possible, there are times that you'll want a swing

to take over rocking duty so you can take a shower or make a sandwich or—if the twinkle-twinkle-little-stars align—take a nap.

3. **A WubbaNub**. I was going to say a *pacifier* here—which, by the way, is totally sufficient—but since we're talking "essentials" instead of essentials, I decided to up the ante a little. A WubbaNub—order one for fifteen bucks on Amazon.com—is a tiny stuffed animal that's sewn to a hospital-grade pacifier. It basically serves to help your baby look supercute as he sucks (something he probably does anyway). But since the animal can sprawl out across your baby's chest, it also helps the pacifier stay in your newborn's mouth—which means there's a better chance of your baby falling asleep with the paci in his mouth instead of waking up and crying when the paci falls on the floor.

4. **A baby bath with a mesh sling**. Sure, the kitchen sink was just fine for you when you were a baby—never mind the super-sharp knives and the baby-foot-sized garbage disposal—but since I'm really going all out with the baby gear luxuries here, I figure it can't hurt to suggest a tiny plastic infant bath. You know: so you can wash your baby and take cute first bath pictures without worrying about him slipping and falling onto sharp utensils. We are an excessive generation, aren't we?

5. **A baby carrier**. I'm actually not super opinionated on the type—I've tried and liked the Baby Björn, the Ergo, a variety of baby slings, and even the Moby wrap. And while each of these has its pros and cons—ask your friends if you want details—the important thing here is that by carrying your baby in some sort of carrier, you get the double bonus of having your hands free to do things like wash dishes or put on makeup while also being able to snuggle and bond with your baby.

6. **A phone with a video camera**. Trust me: you do *not* want to miss it when your baby starts to do ridiculously cute things like lie on a blanket while staring at nothing. And once you've

captured your baby in all of his ridiculously cute cuteness, you're going to need to send that video on to all eighty-four friends on your contact list. Trust me; people love stuff like that. At least your mother-in-law does.

Baby Gear "Essentials" for Three- to Six-Month-Olds

1. **A baby recliner**. Just when you thought you convinced your hubby that the old pea-green recliner he found on the side of the road during his bachelor days isn't appropriate for a household with children, I'm trying to convince you otherwise. But rest assured, it's not what you think. Babies in the three-to-six-month set like to kick back, chill out, and watch you do the things you do. I had a Baby Björn brand bouncy seat with my kids, and I loved it because it folded flat and I could pack it and carry it anywhere I went. My friend Christy said she loved her Boppy Newborn Lounger—which her husband affectionately renamed "the baby's dog bed"—because it was an easy and safe place to plop her babies for a nap.

2. **A stroller**. I used to think the purpose of a stroller was to provide a safe and comfortable place for a baby to sit. But I was wrong. Because I now know that the purpose of a stroller is to hold your purse, your car keys, your cell phone, and your latte—all so they are within easy and convenient reach when you need them. So, as you shop for the ideal stroller, you can just forget about things like padded seats or leg room for baby and focus on the features that really matter—undercarriage space and cup holders. If it has that, you're set.

3. **A high chair**. Once your baby starts eating solid foods, you'll probably have to retire your hold-the-baby-in-my-lap-while-I-shovel-food-in method and spring for a high chair. I have two rules for you when it comes to buying a high chair: (1) Buy something small or—at the very least—foldable. If your high chair takes up more space than your dining room table, you're probably going to start to resent it. (2) Buy something

washable. I don't care how cute the duckie seat with ruffles looks in the store; once it gets smeared with sweet potatoes and strained peas, it will not be cute anymore. It will be stained. Buy something plastic or vinyl that you can wipe down quickly and with one hand.

4. **A video monitor**. I totally made fun of my sister, Alisa, when she bought a video monitor. I sat her down, and after outlining my vast credentials as a baby gear expert, I proceeded to explain to her that she would undoubtedly hear her baby crying if her baby needed her, and that spending her much-needed down time watching her baby sleep was not only ridiculous but a complete waste of time that could be better spent doing something productive, like eating chocolate cake. But Alisa didn't listen to me, and she kept said monitor. And then she had the nerve to let me use said monitor one night while I was babysitting. Of course I set it on the counter and vowed not to look at it. But then I heard her daughter fuss and I took one teeny peek, which progressed into a full-on video monitoring session and ultimately resulted in my forking over two hundred dollars for my own video monitor for my house. It was just so great to be able to spy on my son as he tossed and turned and threw his blankets out of the crib! It was the best two hundred dollars I ever spent on "essential" baby gear.

5. **A smartphone**. You would think that the squeaky, squawky, and loud toys they sell at Target would be a huge hit with your baby. But you would be wrong. Because the only toys that will capture your baby's attention for more than twelve seconds are toys you don't want him to touch. Toys like your iPhone, your remote control, and your straightening iron. So—and here's where your Christian mom savvy will really shine—instead of hiding your iPhone and telling your baby he can't touch it, put it a foot in front of your baby and use it to motivate your baby to learn how to crawl. Smart, right? (Note:

When he actually figures out how to crawl and manages to change the settings and password on your iPhone, you're on your own. You can't expect me to know *everything*.)

Baby Gear "Essentials" for Six- to-Twelve-Month-Olds

1. **An ExerSaucer**. Basically, an ExerSaucer is a seat that is surrounded by various musical and electronic toys that your baby will find fascinating for an exorbitant amount of time. Like fifteen minutes. Which means you'll buy yourself fifteen minutes to do crazy, previously impossible tasks, like unloading the dishwasher or folding laundry. You need one, don't you? Go ask Mr. Google right now. If you order one on Amazon.com with two-day shipping, you could have one in, well, two days.

2. **A push car**. A push-car walker will not only serve to assist you in making hugely popular "my-baby-is-almost-walking" videos to post on Facebook, but may also actually help your baby learn to walk. Of course, whether or not you want him to learn to walk when he is only nine months old is an entirely different issue.

3. **A jogging stroller**. I know I already told you to buy a regular stroller, but once your baby is about six months old, it may be time to pick up a jogging stroller in addition to your other stroller. Because if you have a jogging stroller, you can do really fun things, like go to the park in your workout gear and let everyone assume that the reason you're sweaty and unshowered is because you just finished a ten-mile run.

4. **A convertible car seat**. There will be a day—when your baby is about nine or ten months old—when you'll catch yourself telling your friends that you don't need to go to Pilates because carrying your baby's infant carrier is all the workout you need. And this is a sign that it's time to move your baby up to a convertible seat. Because as much as it's convenient to be able to take your baby in and out of the car in his seat,

it's probably fairly inconvenient to deal with strained arm muscles every time you attempt it.

Getting the Gear You Need

So, basically, in order to be completely prepared for any and every new-baby situation you may encounter, you'll need about fifteen thousand dollars to spend on baby gear, in addition to twenty thousand dollars to remodel your house so you'll have the storage capacity to keep and store all the stuff your baby needs. Simple enough, right? Oh, wait; you don't have thirty-five thousand dollars sitting around? And you don't want to remodel your house to resemble a baby superstore? Neither do I.

With my first baby, I spent way (way) too much money on baby gear. And a lot of my money was wasted when my son used the gear for two months and then never touched it again. So I want to close this chapter by giving you some ideas on how to get the gear you need without having to get a second job. Because trust me: you don't have the energy for that.

10 Ways to Beg, Steal, and Borrow Baby Gear on the Cheap
1. Post a list of the things you'd like to borrow on Facebook. I did this after I had Will and had a borrowed swing within an hour. And some people think Facebook is a time-waster. *Pshaw.*
2. Go to a consignment sale. I scored a $150 Arm's Reach Co-Sleeper for $20 at our MOPS consignment sale and I still brag about it.
3. Go to garage sales.
4. Check Craigslist.com.
5. Ask your friends for hand-me-downs.
6. Ask grandma to buy it.
7. Swap with a friend who has a baby of a different age. You take the ExerSaucer, and she can have the newborn bath.

8. Go to store websites to check their weekly specials.
9. Return the stuff you got at your baby shower that you don't need (read: all twenty-seven adorable-yet-impractical baby outfits) and buy stuff that you do need.
10. Stalk the coupon sites. There's a weekly coupon roundup on Sunday nights on savingwithshellie.com where I find all sorts of good deals on baby gear.

You Can't Always Get What You Want

If the Rolling Stones—well, them and our limited budget—hadn't rained on my baby-gear-buying parade, I would have a houseful of really cool and super-expensive baby gear that I used twelve times and then put into storage. And that would've been really amazing. For twelve minutes. But guess what? I have survived three kids without a Bugaboo stroller. Or a nap nanny. So if the baby-gear buying is really taking a toll on your budget and your sanity, I encourage you to reread this chapter with an eye for the truly essential basics. Because technically, you only really need somewhere for your baby to sleep, somewhere for your baby to poop, something for your baby to travel in, and something for your baby to wear. The rest, well, you can't always get what you want, my friends.

NINE

Medical Helpline

An Invitation to Be a Fly on the Wall at the Pediatrician's Office

Hello! Come on in! I'd like to officially invite you to join me as I spy on the goings-on in a typical pediatrician's office. Oh, wait. That sounds creepy. Let me reassure you that I don't even have the technical know-how to install virus protection software on my computer, so the chances of me actually finding out how to work a bug or phone tap are slim to none. But I do know that moms everywhere—moms like me, who are desperate to make the right health choices for their kids—would just love to have access to quick, easy-to-digest medical information. And I can at least give you a start on getting that info by helping you spy on the medical professionals who—unlike me—actually know what they're talking about when it comes to the health care of your baby.

Now, it probably goes without saying that the medical advice in this book cannot and should not take the place of the advice and expertise of a qualified medical professional that you know and trust. Because your baby's health is too important to trust to a book or an online forum that may be staffed by teenagers in Bermuda. So if you're concerned about your baby's health—for any reason—you should call your pediatrician or nurse practitioner right away.

I keep my doctor's nurses on speed dial and call them quite often. The nurses, Ethel and Natalie (not that I'm on a first-name basis with them or anything), have always proven to be very astute at determining whether my kids just need a hug or a middle-of-the-night doctor's visit. I called them just last night, in fact, after my six-year-old Joey got stung not once, not twice, but three times by scorpions while playing in our kiddie pool. And after a panicked, sobbing phone call to Natalie while I mentally packed our bags for the hospital, I learned that scorpion stings (at least from scorpions in Central Texas) are really no worse than bee stings. Who knew? The fact is that by calling my doctor, I saved myself a lot of panic and possibly a trip to urgent care as my son's leg swelled up and he cried from the pain. About an hour later, after a cool bath, he was just fine.

So my number one and first piece of baby health advice is to call your doctor. That said, if you're just wanting to get the lay of the land when it comes to pediatric care—or get some assurance that that tiny rash that's only on your baby's pinkie toe is really just a tiny spot on your baby's toe and not some rare tropical disease—you've come to the right place.

· ·

Time-Out for Mom

For When You're Praying for Your Baby's Health

"Do not be anxious about anything, but in every situation, by prayer and petition, with thanksgiving, present your requests to God. And the peace of God, which transcends all comprehension, will guard your hearts and your minds in Christ Jesus." (Phillippians 4:6–7)

Lord God, it is so easy to get anxious about my baby's health! I want him to lead a long and healthy life, and it's easy to start to worry when I hear the smallest cough or notice the tiniest ailment. Lord, protect this precious life. Keep him strong and healthy. And give me the peace that comes from trusting You. Amen.

. . . .

The Waiting Room

Before we head back into the back of the office—where the real fun will start—we'll take a short detour into the waiting room. The first thing you may notice is that there is not one, but two waiting rooms—one for sick kids and one for healthy kids. I love this idea in theory because it means that when my kids are just visiting for a well check, I can relax my typical wipe-down-every-possible-surface-my-kids-could-touch-with-Clorox-wipes routine and actually sit and wait in the waiting room.

But like all theoretically good ideas, this one also has a catch: people don't follow the rules. And this drives me crazy. Just last week I was sitting in the safe haven of the well child waiting room, waiting for my son's well check, when I heard a woman's voice from outside the room. She said, "Let's just go into the well-child room so she doesn't pick up anything else. She's sick enough as it is, so I don't want to expose her to any new bugs." I wanted to block her way into the room with a "Listen here, lady. I've spent the last ten minutes anti-bacing my kid's life to keep him from getting sick, and I'm not going to jeopardize my baby's health for your little scheme, so get your little patooty into the sick-kid room and stay there." But I didn't. Instead I grabbed my son and slinked into the hallway and hid from her, all the while praying silently that my doctor would come soon.

My point is that while you may be imagining that the sick-kid waiting room is a regular petri dish full of germs just waiting to crawl onto your baby—and the well-child waiting room is a perfectly germ-free bubble of cleanliness—the truth is that the two rooms probably aren't *that* different. Both have probably had sick kids waiting in them in the last day or two, and both have probably been wiped down with germ-killers in the last day or two. Your best bet is to choose the correct room for your kid (well-child room if your kid is healthy, sick room if your kid is sick), put on some anti-bac gel, and try not to panic too much about your baby being exposed to more germs.

The Weigh Station

The first place you'll stop once the nurse calls you out of germ land is the weighing station. And while you probably dread stepping on Señor Scale when you go to the doctor's office, you'll probably really look forward to your baby's weigh-ins on Señorita Baby Scale. Because while Señor Scale is mean and nasty and always serves to taunt you about the little midnight ice cream binge you had last week, Señorita Baby Scale is actually quite sweet. In fact, she'll give you lots of conversation fodder for the church nursery (can you believe that little Johnny is in the seventy-fifth percentile for both weight and height?), and she'll probably reassure you every time you meet her that that your baby is growing quite nicely.

If you're visiting your pediatrician because your baby is sick, the nurse will probably just have you plop your baby on the scale fully dressed in order to get an approximate weight. This is mostly done so your doctor can accurately prescribe medicine in the correct dosage.

But if you're in the doctor's office for a well check, your time with Señorita Baby Scale will be a bit more extensive. A typical scenario will most likely involve the nurse measuring your baby's head size with a round tape-measure thing to make sure your baby's skull is developing properly, and then measuring your baby's height with a flat tape measure to make sure he's growing up as well as out. This can be tricky. At my son Will's nine-month well check, he was kicking and rolling and wriggling so badly that it took both me and the nurse to hold him down. The struggle must have put a kink in the measuring tape, because when the doctor checked the height measurements we got against the growth chart and he showed up in the 145th percentile (when he'd always been average in height), we knew there was a mistake. Turns out we had the measurement wrong by more than three inches.

Once the nurse checks your baby's height, the real fun will begin. It will start with a simple request: "Can you please strip your baby down, diaper and all, so I can get an accurate weight measurement?" Key words: Diaper. And. All. As you take off your baby's socks and then his little Onesie, your heartbeat will speed up and your body will go into fight-or-flight mode as it prepares for the mad dash to get your baby on and off the scale and back into his diaper without him peeing all over you, the nurse, and the cute little teddy bear poster that some naive person hung right above the scale. And if your baby is anything like mine—especially my boys (although my daughter has had her share of pee-on-the-scale incidents)—you'll fail miserably. Because there is something about the freedom of going diaper-less in a new place and the cold air of the pediatrician's office that's, well, let's say *inspiring*.

Of course, the nurse will have a container of wipes nearby for you to sop up the mess and restore Señorita Baby Scale to her previous clean state. At least until the next baby pees all over her. Then you can head back into the exam rooms and get ready to see the doctor.

The Well Check

Going to your baby's well check will probably be the one and only time you actually look forward to visiting the pediatrician. Because not only will your doc give you (I mean, your baby) a sticker and—if you're really good—a lollipop, she'll also give you insight into all the amazing ways your baby is developing, growing, and learning.

The visit will probably start with a quick Q & A session, where your doctor will ask you what your baby is doing and how she is eating and pooping. And while you may be tempted to rattle off some facts about how your baby is already enrolled in Baby Mandarin classes and doing calisthenics with a personal trainer, that is totally unnecessary. The doctor isn't asking all these questions to try to figure out if you should be nominated for the mom-of-the-year award (you should) but instead to make sure your baby is doing, eating, and pooping all the things he should be doing, eating, and pooping for a baby his age.

Once your doctor checks on some basics, she'll check out your baby from head to toe. This will most likely involve checking your baby's eyes, ears, throat, hips, diaper area, and stomach, just to make sure everything is in tip-top shape. Then your doctor may ask your baby to perform some tricks—things like lifting his head, sitting up on his own, clapping, waving, babbling, or standing. This can be a source of pride—my son Will loves to show off for the doctor, and the second she says something like, "Can you wave bye-bye?" he'll paste on a ten-thousand-dollar grin and wave like a Hollywood movie star. Yep. My baby is the most advanced waver in town. And my doctor has proof.

My son Joey? Not so much. He's six. And seeing as how he has an entire year of kindergarten under his belt, I'm fairly certain he knows how to wave. But I can pretty much guarantee that if the doctor asked him to wave bye-bye, he'd look at her blankly as if she were asking him to solve the quadratic formula. Because he's not one to show off for the doctor. And that's okay too. Because while your pediatrician certainly cares that your baby is able to do things like lift up his head, sit up, clap, wave, babble, and stand, your pediatrician also will believe you that your baby can do it at home—even if he won't perform in the office. *Whew.*

After your baby's performance (er, check) the doctor will probably address your questions (no, you don't need to worry that Lil' Miss Thing hasn't started saying, "Unicorn" by six months) and concerns (yes, it's fine that Junior's poop ranges from yellow to brown) and then send you on your way. Well, almost on your way. There's still one little thing to deal with: vaccines.

Vaccines

The last thing that will (most likely) happen at your baby's well check is your baby will get his vaccines. Now, I'm not even going to get into the vaccine debate right now, partly because I'm not a doctor and I don't feel I can speak authoritatively, but mostly because I don't want to get a bunch of hate mail in my in-box. And, to put it lightly, giving your opinion about vaccines in the company of parents is comparable to giving your opinion about Google Plus in the company of technophobes. You. Don't. Want. To. Go. There.

I will tell you, however, that there are lots of people who have lots of opinions about vaccines. And while I can't give you comprehensive information about normal vaccination schedules versus delayed vaccination schedules versus I'm-going-to-go-it-on-my-own-and-hope-everyone-else-vaccinates schedules, I will tell you one thing: stay off the Internet. Mr. Google is not a reliable source when it comes to the vaccine debate. Yes, there is a lot of great information out there, but there are also lots of crazy loonies (sorry) who will rant and rave and tell untrue or half-true stories about vaccines. Your best bet when making decisions about whether and how to vaccinate your baby is to—you guessed it—talk to your doctor.

If you do decide to vaccinate (which I did; don't hate), your baby will get a few shots at nearly every well check during his first year of life. This is very traumatic—for you, at least. Your baby will probably hardly feel it. That said, it can't hurt to give your baby a little infant Tylenol to ease the pain beforehand or distract him with a paci dipped in sugar water (your doctor probably has some; all you have to do is ask). The bribing-with-sugar strategy works well at all ages, so may as well start him out young. I'm kidding. Sort of.

But really, chances are your baby will cry for a max of three minutes—time it if you don't believe me—and then you can get him dressed, get your (I mean, your *baby's*) lollipop, and be on your way.

Common Baby Ailments

I hate to break it to you, but even if you've managed to place an industrial-sized bottle of anti-bac gel at eye level in every room and you accost every person who gets within five feet of your baby to wash their hands, your baby is still going to get sick. And while having a sick baby is totally sad and will probably make you want to pack up your stuff and move into a germ-free bubble for the rest of his childhood, I want to reassure you that most likely you both will be just fine. Really. Here are a few of the most common baby ailments you may see in the first year:

- **Ear infections**. My son Will has had, like, a billion ear infections (or maybe like seven) in the past few months—and I always know he has another one when he gets fussy while he's nursing. Normally he loves his milk, but it must hurt for him to lie down in that position when his little ears are infected because, without fail, that's the first sign that I need to take him in. Your baby may also start pulling on his ears, waking up at night, or fussing when you lay him down.
- **Colds and runny noses**. You can go ahead and trust me that while you may be swearing to yourself right now that your kid will never have crusty snot caked on his face like everyone else's babies, by the end of that first cold season, you will learn to look right past the constant drip of your baby's nose. You also won't blink before you wipe your baby's nose on his sleeve, your sleeve, or whatever other

semisoft absorbent material you have available. Because you're a mom. And that's what moms do.

- ᴄ⟋ᴏ **Fever**. Fevers can be scary—especially in newborns. My daughter, Kate, earned herself a weeklong stay at the children's hospital when she was two weeks old because of a measly 100.8 fever. In the end she was just fine, but the doctors took it very seriously. As a general rule, if your baby is under two months old and has a fever over 100.4, head to the ER right away. If your baby is older than two months and has a fever, call your doctor but don't head to the ER just yet.
- ᴄ⟋ᴏ **Thrush**. Thrush is actually totally and completely painless to your baby—which is good—but it can be really painful for a breast-feeding mom. Basically it's a yeast infection in the baby's mouth that results in a mom's nipples getting very, very sore. If you're struggling to breast-feed due to sore nipples—especially if you've made it past the initial two weeks of breast-feeding or the pain went away and then came back, check the inside of your baby's mouth. If you see a white coating that looks like milk that you can't wipe off, call your doctor.
- ᴄ⟋ᴏ **Vomiting**. Your baby will probably spit up—even spit up entire feedings—from time to time. And that's totally normal. But if your baby suddenly spews vomit that lands all the way across the room and splatters up the wall, that's not. You should probably call your doctor. The actual vomiting is probably not a problem, but babies are little and can get dehydrated really fast, so it's important to be proactive in keeping your baby hydrated.
- ᴄ⟋ᴏ **Diarrhea**. Diarrhea in babies is a bit tricky to diagnose because all (or most) baby poop is soft and can be liquidy. The way you know if your baby's diarrhea is worrisome is if the sheer volume increases. Like if you go from three dirty diapers a day to fifteen, you should probably call your doctor.

- **Croup**. Croup is probably the only baby illness you'll be able to diagnose without your doctor's help. If you hear what sounds like a sea lion barking in your baby monitor, your baby has croup. The barking sound is unmistakable—and while it sounds horrible, it's actually not super scary. The best cure is to hop into a nice steamy shower with your baby (or sit in the bathroom with the door shut and the shower on) and hold him while letting him breathe in the hot, steamy air. One caveat: if you hear your baby making stridor noise (sounds like "bark, bark, bark, whheeeee!), you should call your doctor right away.

- **Colic**. The official definition of colic is "a healthy, well-fed infant who cries for more than three hours per day, for more than three days per week, for more than three weeks." (Thank you, WebMD.com.) Yep, it basically means your baby is crying. A lot. And—here's the kicker—there's absolutely nothing you've done or are doing to cause the crying. While it's probably reassuring that your baby is completely fine and that you're not making some terrible mistake as you deal with your baby's constant crying, it's also frustrating to realize there is not much you can do to stop it. So grab some earplugs and a baby sling and carry on, my friend. And don't forget to ask someone to take a turn with your baby when you're feeling overwhelmed. The good news is that colic almost always disappears in the first few months of life.

- **Jaundice**. If you want a technical explanation, jaundice is caused by a spike in bilirubin—a chemical that breaks down red blood cells in your body—in your baby's bloodstream. That said, you may notice your baby's skin turning yellow (or getting yellower) during his first few days of life. Your doctor will definitely be on the lookout for this, but if his skin looks yellow to you, you should still call your doctor just to be on the safe side. In some extreme cases, your baby may have to have blue-light phototherapy. I'm honestly totally clueless as to how this works, but the gist is that you put your baby in a miniature tanning bed–like contraption, and the lights help remove bilirubin from his bloodstream. The marvels of modern medicine, eh?

ER Trips in the Middle of the Night

My girlfriends and I joke (okay, seriously contemplate) that if we could just befriend a doctor—preferably an ER doctor or pediatrician—it would sure make things convenient . . . for us, at least. Instead of back-and-forth worrying about whether to head to the ER when our babies are sick, we could just drag our doctor friend out of bed in the middle of the night and ask her to tell us what to do. Plus, I don't know about everyone else, but I'd feel much more secure on park playdates and bike rides if I had a doctor along. So if any of you pediatricians out there are looking for a totally mutually beneficial friendship, my e-mail address is erin@christianmamasguide.com. I'm really fun. I promise.

Of course, the next best thing to having a doctor for your best friend forever is having a real live doctor give you the 4-1-1 on baby care. I took careful notes last year when ER doctor Jeremy Gabrysch came to our MOPS group and coached us on how to tell the difference between true head-to-the-ER-at-two-in-the-morning emergencies and your-kid-just-has-ketchup-on-his-hand fake-outs.

Jeremy did walk us through all the reasons we should—and shouldn't—go to the ER, but I think the most reassuring thing he said was that doctors expect to get phone calls from worried parents. And that anytime you're in doubt, you can and should pick up the phone and call—because it's always better to double-check than to spend the whole night worrying or to put your baby's health at risk. He also reassured us that a lot of the ailments that absolutely terrify parents—like high fevers and big bumps—are rarely emergencies.

Anyway, if you're just dying to have a check sheet for your fridge, like mine, then you should probably go make friends with a doctor, because I'm not sharing mine. Just kidding. Even though this list is not comprehensive, it has helped me know how to determine the difference between a true emergency and a worried-mom moment.

Reasons to Head to the ER in the Middle of the Night

- Your baby under two months old has a fever over 100.4.
- Your baby lost consciousness after a fall.
- Your baby is vomiting repeatedly after a fall.
- Your baby bonked his head, and the bump goes in instead of out.
- Your baby has a seizure.
- Your baby is vomiting and/or has diarrhea and hasn't had a wet diaper in eight hours.
- Your baby is lethargic or unresponsive.
- Your baby has a broken bone that is sticking out of the skin or his arm or leg is hanging at a strange angle.
- Your baby has a cut on his face that is bleeding severely.
- Your baby has a cut anywhere on his body and you can't control the bleeding.
- Your baby has a rash that looks like tiny purple pinpricks.

Reasons to Call Your Doctor in the Middle of the Night (But Don't Head to the ER Just Yet)

- Your baby bonked his head, and the bump is the size of a grapefruit . . . but otherwise he seems fine.
- Your baby, between two and six months old has a fever over 100.5.
- Your baby over six months old has a fever over 103.

The Christian Mama's Guide to Baby's First Year

- Your baby is vomiting nonstop and unable to keep anything down.
- Your baby has a cut but you have controlled the bleeding.

Did I Mention That I'm Not a Doctor?

One last thing before we move on to talk about something a bit more fun—have I mentioned that I'm not a doctor? And that all of the medical-ish advice in this chapter can't *ever* substitute for the advice of a well-trained medical professional who knows you, knows your baby, and—perhaps most important—knows what she is talking about? So take everything I said with a giant grain of salt, and check everything I said—and everything you'll read on Mr. Google—against whatever your doctor tells you. And if your doctor and I disagree—listen to your doctor. Because as much as I hate to admit this, she probably knows a bit more than I do.

TEN

It's Playtime

Having Fun with Your Baby

A typical day in mommy-of-baby land: wake up; nurse the baby; make a mug of coffee and carefully sip it while standing at the kitchen counter, watching your baby lie on a blanket on the floor and stare at toys; make breakfast; eat breakfast while the baby lies on the floor on a blanket and stares at toys; read every book on your baby's bookshelf to your baby while he drools on your lap; make another cup of coffee; drink said coffee while your baby lies on a blanket on the floor and bats at toys; go on a walk with the stroller; nurse the baby; put the baby down for a nap; frantically take a shower; dry your hair; throw in a load of laundry; and sweep up the sugar you dumped all over the floor while making coffee, because you were rushing to get into the living room to watch your baby lying on the floor.

But then eight forty-five hits. And your baby wakes up from his nap and is raring to go, and you've already had enough of your usual watch-the-baby-while-he-stares-at-toys routine for the rest of the day. What do you do all day with a baby who can't even move? Or a baby who can move, but the only thing he moves toward are things like electrical outlets or four-hundred-dollar iPhones? And how do you utilize your time to help your baby learn not only about how to live and love life, but also how to live and love Jesus?

Keeping Busy with Your Baby

I probably shouldn't say something like this in writing—especially when I'm talking to a bunch of new moms—but sometimes being a mom is boring. There. I said it. Now, I know there are lots of highs—times when you're witness to that first smile or those first steps—times when you just can't pull the camera out fast enough. There are also lots of sweet, tender moments when your baby is snuggled close and you can't imagine doing anything else than what you are doing right then. But there are also lots of hours when you're stuck at home, unsure of what to do to keep your baby busy and yourself sane. Here are a few ideas:

10 Things to Do with Your Newborn
1. Lay your newborn faceup on your lap, and give him a foot massage. Use baby lotion to make it really soothing.
2. Set your baby in a bouncer, and let him watch you do an exercise video. You'll get some exercise, and he'll get the fun of watching you jump around and dance for him.
3. Babies love to be close to you, so let him ride in a baby carrier or sling while you make dinner, put on your makeup, or go for a walk.
4. Lie down next to your baby on a blanket, and rub his back while you sing hymns or favorite songs.
5. Young babies love patterns that contrast, so walk around your house together, and explore all the places you can see black against white, brown against cream, or navy against yellow. Point them out.

6. Hold a mirror about a foot in front of your baby's face, and let him stare at his own face.

7. Make silly noises or sing nonsense songs to your baby to see if you can get him to laugh. My friend Ben's baby giggled hilariously every time his parents sang "Baby Got Back"—and so, much to his mother-in-law's chagrin, they got very good at singing that song.

8. If your baby is a little fussy or gassy, set him on his back and do bicycle legs, crisscross his arms, and do tummy massages. My husband affectionately coined any sort of baby manipulation—you know: when you gently make their legs or arms move—the Toot Olympics. Things like bicycle legs never failed to help Joey relieve some of his gassiness.

9. Give your baby a bath, and let him chill out in the warm water.

10. If your baby is a good sport, pose him on a plain-colored blanket in a variety of different hats for a regular Anne Geddes–style photo shoot. So what if your photos don't turn out like a professional's? You'll still have great memories from the time you took them.

10 Things to Do with Your Baby Once He Can Sit Up

1. Gather up some of your scarves (or scraps of fabric or dish towels) and then flutter them around your baby. Throw them into the air and let them drop on his head or brush them across his skin.

2. Play peekaboo, but instead of standing in one place, hide around corners or behind cabinets, and then pop out in front of your baby.

3. Set out a beach towel and sit together outside and read books, play with toys, or just enjoy the sunshine. (Just don't forget the sunscreen!)

4. Make like a rock star and make musical instruments out of pots, pans, and spoons.

5. Pull out your old photo albums and show him the pictures,

explaining who each person is and what you're doing. It'll be fun for you to walk down memory lane and fun for him to see pictures of the people—Daddy, Grandma, Auntie Margaret—he's grown to know and love.

6. Make a mixed tape of your favorite old songs, and sing at the top of your lungs while sashaying around the house with your baby in your arms.

7. Fill your bathtub up with bath toys—but no water—and plop your baby into the tub, clothes and all. (Note: Even if you're watching vigilantly, make sure you have a safety lock on the faucet and a foam pad on the spout.)

8. Head out to your car and sit on your front seat while your baby stands in your lap and pretends to drive.

9. Go on a tour of your house. Grab your baby and walk around the house, talking about each room and all the things you do there. Make sure to point out things that you know your baby loves. "Oh! There's your high chair, where you eat all those yummy smooshed peas!" and "Look! There's the door that Daddy comes through when he gets home from work."

10. Go on a stroller walk. As you walk down the street, point out the trees, the birds, the clouds, and the cars to your baby.

10 Things to Do with Your Crawling, Creeping, and Walking Baby

1. Set your baby's high chair outside (or in some other place where you're not worried about the floor getting wet), and then fill the tray with about a quarter inch of water. Strip him down to his diaper, give him a few teaspoons, and let him splash and play in the water.

2. Buy some chunky crayons—my kids all loved the pyramid-shaped ones made for babies—and hold your baby's hand in your own as you show him how crayons work. (Don't worry if your baby spends more time trying to eat crayons than color with them. That's why they make them nontoxic.)

3. Turn your living room into a bubble disco. Pick up some

soap-free glycerin bubbles (the soapy ones can sting your baby's eyes) and then turn on some dance tunes and blow bubbles, dancing with your baby as the bubbles float around the room.

4. Let your baby baby you. Put a pillow on the floor and say you're going to bed. Sing a lullaby together and help him snuggle a blanket, over you. Then reverse the process and see if he'll pretend to go night-night.

5. Put a blanket over a kiddie table and let your baby crawl inside his "fort" to play.

6. Go on a wild blankie ride. Plop him (belly-side down) on a favorite blanket, and then pull him around the room.

7. Get an empty box (a jumbo-sized diaper box is perfect) and put a few toys in it. Let your baby figure out how to knock the box over and then crawl inside to get the toys.

8. Chop up a variety of fruits, veggies, cheeses, and other foods, and feed them to your baby one at a time to see what he likes and dislikes.

9. Take a cue from a kindergarten teacher and do center time with your baby. Spend five minutes looking at books, then five minutes playing with stuffed animals, then five minutes knocking over blocks. By the time your baby starts to get bored with one toy, he'll have already moved on to the next.

10. Go outside (put your baby in your sling or a Björn) and collect leaves, blades of grass, or flower petals. Then sit with your baby as you look at each item you collected, describing the shape, texture, and colors.

Toys That Aren't Toys

When I started writing this chapter, I sent an e-mail out to my friends and asked them about their babies' favorite toys. And while I got the occasional "ExerSaucer" or "Baby Einstein radio," the vast majority of my friends' responses were things like rubber spatulas, Tupperware containers, and remote controls. And this is a very cool thing. Because the way I look at it, the less cash you spend on noisy, flashing, electronic toys, the more cash you have to spend on things like date nights with your husband. That, and you'll save your sanity. (Because trust me: once your baby figures out that a toy beeps whenever you press that tiny orange button, he will press that tiny orange button. Again. And again. And again.)

Here are a few ideas for toys you can find (or make) with things you probably already have at your house.

- **A busy box**. Grab a shoebox (if you're feeling really ambitious, pick up one of those plastic shoeboxes at Target so it will withstand drool) and fill it with various "toys" for your baby. As a general rule, anything that can fit through the center of a toilet paper roll is a choking hazard (or has parts that small), but anything bigger than that is fair game. In my busy box, I put an empty water bottle (without the screw-on top), an old scrap of fur from my sewing box, a scarf, a couple of small balls, an old remote control (batteries removed), and a board book. Anytime I needed my kids to stay busy (say, when I really, really needed to check my e-mail), I pulled out the busy box and handed it to them (after much to-do, singing, "Ooooh, what's in my busy box? [*Shake shake!*] Oh what's in my busy box?" in order to get them interested).
- **Laundry baskets**. Set your baby inside a laundry basket—think a boat out of the water—and sing sailing songs.
- **Pots, pans, and Tupperware**. Letting your baby play with kitchen implements isn't a new idea—I bet your mom did it when you were a kid. But to make sure your spaghetti pot isn't covered in baby slobber when you need it, my suggestion is to choose one (small) cupboard and fill it with

a few "toys"—smaller pots, plastic bowls, metal strainers—that you don't mind your baby playing with. Don't put a child lock on that cabinet, so your baby can open and close the door with ease. He'll figure out pretty quickly which cabinet he can get into, and you'll save yourself the hassle of loading pots and pans in and out of the cupboard every time you're cooking dinner.

- **Empty soap bottles**. You know that Mango Tango shower gel that you've been using as slowly as possible because you really don't want to have to drag your baby to the store to buy more? Use it up, girl! Once it's gone, toss the lid (it's a choking hazard), rinse out the container and then set it aside for your baby to play with when you're drying your hair or putting on your makeup. Once you have a little collection of bottles, your baby will have a lot of fun rolling them across the floor, stacking them on top of each other, and—the big attraction—sucking on them like lollipops.
- **Boxes**. Set out a variety of boxes—everything from the giant diaper box you just finished off to the tiny shoebox that your baby's first Jordans came in. Let your baby open and close the boxes, fill them with toys, climb inside them, and push them around the room.

Learning about Jesus

I want my babies to grow up knowing that Jesus is and will always be the centerpiece of their lives. So I want our playtime to also be a time that they can learn about Jesus. But it's hard! Not because I don't believe that Jesus is the most important thing I can teach them about—but because a small baby simply doesn't have the capacity to grasp huge concepts like faith and redemption and grace. But that doesn't mean you can't let Jesus shine through the games you play and the books you read—because every time you teach your baby something about Jesus, it brings him one step closer to knowing Him on a personal level.

· ·

Time-Out for Mom

For When You're Praying for Your Baby's Spiritual Growth

"When they had finished eating, Jesus said to Simon Peter, 'Simon son of John, do you love me more than these?'

'Yes, Lord,' he said, 'you know that I love you.'

Jesus said, 'Feed my lambs.'" (John 21:15)

Jesus, the best way I can show my love for You is to feed Your lambs. And You have given me one of your precious little lambs to steward, and I pray that I will be able to give my baby what he needs to thrive spiritually. Give me the patience, insight, and will to raise him in a way that honors You and leads him toward a saving faith. Amen.

· ·

Activities That Will Teach Your Baby about Jesus

1. Set your baby on his back on a blanket—this is a perfect thing to do outside if the sun isn't too bright—and spend a few minutes praying over each part of his body. Grab his toes and say, "Thank You, Jesus, for creating these adorable little piggies! May they one day run to spread Your gospel to those who need it most." Or gently rub his head and say, "Thank You, Jesus, for this precious baby of mine! Make him and mold him into what You want him to be."

2. Play Noah's ark. You can pick up a Noah's ark set, complete with a wooden boat and animals at any toy store—or just

grab a few of your baby's stuffed animals, and a box and ad lib. As your baby plays with the boat and the animals, talk to him about God's plan for redemption and how He saved Noah because he was righteous. Don't forget to throw in several rounds of the "Arky-Barky" song—if you don't know the words, you'd better learn them fast, as this is a parenting essential for the Vacation Bible School set.

3. Explore God's creation. Take your baby on a walk in a stroller or baby carrier, and as you walk, talk about God's incredible creation and the beauty He has surrounded us with in order to show His great love. Sure, your baby may not grasp exactly what you're talking about (yet), but he will love looking around at the trees, the clouds, and the flowers and hearing your voice as you talk.

4. Get a stuffed sheep and teach your baby to take care of the sheep by touching it gently and giving it hugs. Then talk to your baby about how Jesus is our Shepherd and always takes care of us with a gentle and loving touch.

Age-Appropriate Books That Will Teach Your Baby about Jesus

I'm sure you've heard all of the propaganda (er, research) that reading to babies is the best way to grow their vocabulary and jump-start language skills, basically ensuring that they grow up to be literate, book-reading citizens. Now, don't get me wrong—I love books—but there were times when my kids were babies that I wondered exactly what they were gaining from our little use-the-book-as-a-teething-toy-while-mommy-tries-to-read-to-you sessions. Because the truth was, my kids never seemed to absorb a word. And worse, our reading sessions often ended in a tantrum when my kids were more interested in tearing out the pages and chewing on the spine than actually listening to the story.

But here's the thing: your baby *is* listening. Even if he appears to be arching his back and throwing a fit because he wants to get down and play with his toys, he's still listening. And there will be a day when you realize that all those hours spent reading actually did something. Just a few weeks ago, my one-year-old, Will, pointed to a dog and said, "Woof!" I wondered how he knew that, since I had never taught him animal sounds—but then I remembered *Moo, Baa, La! La! La!* (by Sandra Boynton) talks all about how dogs say, "Woof!" And my little literary genius made the connection—all by himself. I was so proud.

Anyway, reading is a great activity to do with your baby—and it's even more special when you can read stories that teach your baby about Jesus. Here are some of my favorite Christian books for babies:

- *Thank You, God, for Loving Me* by Max Lucado
- *Really Wooly Bedtime Prayers* by Dayspring
- *The Story of Jesus* by Roger Priddy
- *Jesus Hears Me* by Joni Walker
- *Baby Jesus* by Caroline Church
- *Thank You, God* by P. K. Hallinan
- *Night Night Blessings* by Amy Parker
- *Annie Ant, Don't Cry!* by Sigmund Brouwer
- Light My World series by Thomas Kinkade
- *You Are Special* by Max Lucado

(Note: You may have noticed the conspicuous lack of a Bible or children's Bible on this list. This is not because I don't like reading the Bible to my kids—in fact, Joey and Kate's all-time favorite book is *The Jesus Storybook Bible* by Sally Lloyd-Jones—but for your baby, your trusty King James may be a bit over his head. Plus, if your babies are anything like mine, there is a good chance they'll tear out the pages as quickly as you can read them. So I limited this list to board books, knowing that as your baby grows, the Bible will become an essential part of his library.)

Just Hanging Out

I'm a doer—I have to be doing something at all times. Which means the idea of sitting on a blanket and just relaxing with my baby is really hard for me. And I start to think about how I'd be a better mom if only I could plan next week's Sunday school lesson while knitting a scarf and teaching my baby Mandarin. Simultaneously, of course. This drives my laid-back, I-could-care-less-if-there-are-dishes-in-the-sink husband crazy, and he's constantly reminding me that spending an hour lying on a blanket, snuggling with our baby, is just that—spending a relaxing and wonderful hour lying on a blanket and bonding with my precious baby, who will grow up way, way too fast.

I want to remind you type A, must-plan-something-to-fill-up-every-moment-of-the-day moms like me that it's okay to leave parts of your day unscripted. Your baby needs you—and time with you—not educational activities and kinesthetic lessons. And your days as a mom aren't measured in how many loads of laundry you fold or how many times you sweep the floor, but how much time you spend investing in what matters most. Okay, sappy reminder over. Now wipe those tears off your face and let's talk about something else.

ELEVEN

Out On the Town

*Getting out of the House
with Your Baby*

D on't listen to all those closed-minded people who tell you that leaving the house with baby is sometimes more trouble than it's worth. Because those are the same people who consider it work to pack up a baby along with 13,493 pieces of baby equipment and lug everything into the car only to spend three minutes in the grocery store. They obviously aren't thinking clearly. Maybe they have the dreaded mommy brain or something. Because going out on the town is easy. And fun. And takes hardly any foresight or planning or packing at all.

Or maybe I'm the one with mommy brain. (Another possibility is that I have a tendency to skip out on all the packing and planning and strategizing and then end up at the park with three kids and no diapers, wipes, or sippy cups.) But I digress. I think most moms would tell you that it's tough to load your baby up into the car or the stroller and head out on the town. But they'd also tell you that the lure of entertainment that doesn't involve your hair dryer and a pack of Cheerios will tempt even the most home-body-ish mamas out of hiding and into the real world.

And since I think it's easy-peasy to pack up and get out the door with three children in tow (see: mommy brain), I put together a checklist to help you get on your way. Just check off the items as you go and you'll be out the door in no time—or at least within the next two hours.

Going Out with Baby Checklist

_____ Feed the baby.

_____ Change the baby's diaper and get him dressed.

_____ Make yourself a cup of coffee (so you'll be energized enough to actually do something when you finally get out of the house).

_____ Change the baby's clothes, because he dumped the dog's water bowl all over himself while you were making coffee.

_____ Load your baby into the car and strap him into his car seat.

_____ Get into the car. Glance in the rearview mirror and notice that you forgot to not only brush your teeth but also comb your hair and put on a bra.

_____ Take your baby out of the car seat and bring him back inside.

_____ Quickly wipe yourself down with a washcloth, paying special attention to the spot where your baby spit up on your shirt three nights ago.

_____ Put on a bra.

_____ Change your baby's clothes because he dumped the dog's water bowl all over himself while you were "showering."

_____ Load your baby into the car and strap him into his car seat.

_____ Pull out of the driveway and get halfway down the street before you realize that you forgot the diaper bag. Spend five minutes analyzing whether it would be quicker to go home and get it or to just go to the mini-mart and buy a super-expensive bag of diapers.

_____ Decide to treat yourself to a mochachino with the money you would've spent on buying super-expensive diapers at the mini-mart. Turn around and head home.

_____ Take your baby out of the car seat and bring him back inside.

_____ Find the diaper bag and give yourself a pat on the back for remembering to check to make sure there were diapers, wipes, and a change of clothes inside.

_____ Change your baby's clothes because he dumped the dog's water bowl all over himself while you were packing his diaper bag.

_____ Load your baby into his car seat. For the final time. For real, this time.

Mothers of Preschoolers

One of my favorite get-out-of-the-house mommy outings is going to Mothers of Preschoolers (MOPS). Ironically, I actually didn't sign up for the MOPS group at my church right after Joey was born because I was adamantly and absolutely certain I wasn't a MOPS kind of mom. I had seen what went on in those meetings—there was a little too much glittering, gluing, and scrapbooking for my taste. But when Joey was about four months old, my friend Rachel convinced me to try just one meeting. And I discovered that I had been very wrong. Because while there was some glittering, gluing, and scrapbooking, there were also moms just like me who understood exactly what I was going through. MOPS became my friendship circle and mommy break and excuse to totally indulge in super-fattening treats like muffins and coffee cake. Because calories eaten at MOPS totally don't count. At least that's what my mentor mom said.

I look forward to MOPS every week. In the six years I've been part of MOPS, I've built camaraderie with my small group and my mentor mom that goes deeper than your average meet-at-the-playground-for-an-hour friendship. My MOPS girls get me. And they love me anyway. It's priceless. And grace-giving and sanity-saving and probably the best thing I've done for myself since becoming a mom. Have I convinced you yet? Good. Now go to MOPS.org to find a local chapter—there's probably one near you—and check it out. Don't let the glitter deter you.

10 Things I've Learned at MOPS . . . That I
Would've Never Learned Otherwise

1. A good dose of sympathetic support is worth far more than a bunch of parenting advice. Even if it's good parenting advice.
2. I'm not the only mom who sometimes wonders if I need therapy. Or at least a good, long vacation.
3. It's okay if my house doesn't always look like a page from the Pottery Barn catalog. Pottery Barn Kids is just fine.
4. Praying for someone is one of the most powerful things I can do.
5. I'm still a good mom even if I never learn how to fold a fitted sheet.
6. My kids can survive in child care for two hours. On their own. Without me checking on them.
7. It's okay to turn off my iPhone for a few hours and focus on talking to real people in real life.
8. There's very little in the world that tastes better than a cup of coffee that I can sip slowly without worrying about anyone knocking it out of my hands.
9. Even the mom who looks completely pulled together—the one who shows up at MOPS with her daughter's hair in french braids and her son wearing clean underwear—isn't necessarily as pulled together as she looks.
10. Mommy friends are better than Facebook friends.

Time-Out for Mom

For When You're Building Mommy Friendships

"As iron sharpens iron, so one person sharpens another."
(Proverbs 27:17)

Almighty God, in the last few months, it seems like everything in my life has changed. But not Your faithfulness. I thank You for being faithful to provide strong, Christian women who are also moms and know the ups and downs of raising a baby. I pray that as my friendships grow, we will strengthen each other through wise words, a listening ear, and selfless love. Help me to be a friend that leads the people I encounter toward You. Amen.

At the Park

I was scared of the park when Joey was a baby. Not only were there clearly posted signs that the park was designed for kids much older than mine (seriously, doesn't anyone follow rules anymore?), but also, I knew the park just had to be positively swimming with germs and dirt and grime. Oh, and there's one more thing: the big kids. Every park I ever saw had big, scary kids—three-year-olds at least—running around like MMA fighters looking for a baby to body slam. I avoided the park like the plague.

I had to face my fears when my MOPS group decided to have a playdate at the local park. The nerve. I wasn't going to go, but then I was having one of those days where Joey wasn't even laughing at my VeggieTales impersonations. And the fact that not only was I acting like an asparagus stalk, but my baby wasn't even cracking a smile at my stellar efforts, made me realize that I had to get out of the house. So I went. Scary big kids and all.

About five minutes into our first park excursion, I did a total about-face. The park was fun! Spending some time in the fresh air with actual adults to talk to was pretty much the best thing that had happened to me. In a long time. (See: Veggie Tales impersonations.) And Joey was having all kinds of fun licking the swings, eating pea gravel, and playing in the mud puddle at the bottom of the slide. Of course, those ginormous three-year-olds were still totally and utterly terrifying—but no place is perfect. And what can you expect? Their moms couldn't exactly trust them at home alone. They could body slam the dog or something.

Anyway, going to the park is still one of my go-to standbys. It's free, it's fun, and I get to meet all sorts of other parents who are just as eager to talk about baby sleep schedules and butt paste as I am. Plus, remember in my pregnancy book when I told you about all the fun people you'd encounter at your childbirth class? Well, guess what? Those people have grown up and had babies too. And they are all waiting for you at the park.

Types of People You May Encounter at the Park

- **The Wheatgrass-Fed Organimommy.** Organimommy has now graduated from kale chips and quinoa bars to superfoods, like acai smoothies and Samba shakes. And she brings her concoctions to the park in handwoven bottles that she makes herself in her backyard while her baby is taking French lessons. The good news is that she always has a picnic lunch packed and she's willing to share. The bad news is that you won't find any Goldfish crackers or Mint Milanos in her cooler.
- **The Frat Guy.** Apparently frat guy's wife has convinced him that it would be a good idea to take the baby to the park for a few hours so she can get a mani-pedi. She must have conveniently forgotten that he needs supervision at all hours of the day or he might do something like stage a

milk-chugging contest at the top of the slide and then rig the contest to make sure his baby would win.

- **The Type A Supermommy**. So this mom doesn't actually have a baby . . . yet. She's about eight weeks pregnant but she's in the process of visiting every park in town and rating each one on a sliding scale according to safety, visibility, and stroller accessibility. She has her stroller in hand—with a watermelon in it to mimic a baby's weight— and she's practicing loading and unloading "her baby" and her stuff in and out of the car while she scopes out the scene. You might want to stay away—being friends with a supermommy is probably more pressure than you can handle right now. But if you can, try to swipe her spreadsheet. Knowing the playground-to-bathroom ratio at all local parks could really come in handy.

- **The Scared-to-Death-of-Everything Mommy**. Remember that mom who was so scared of pain at your childbirth class that her husband had to take her into the hall during the breast-feeding demonstration? Well, now she's at the park. And she has a kid. So if you hear a loud squeal and an "Oh my gosh, he's going to fall!" coming from her mouth, you'll probably find that her son has done something daredevil-ish, like crawl up on the first step of the play area. Don't worry. If he does fall off that one-foot step and land in the soft grass, she has a first aid kit in her diaper bag. Better safe than sorry.

- **The I'm-SO-Excited-and-I-Just-Can't-Hide-It Mommy**. Can you even bee-leeve what a gorgeous day it is? And we are just so lucky that we get to be at the park with our bay-bees today! *Ohmygoodnessgravysakesalive*, do you see how cute little Sarah looks in her brand-spanking-new dress that Grandma sent? Best. Day. Ever.

- **The Public-Displays-of-Adoration Couple**. These two— well, they had the great idea to combine baby time and date night and go on one big sticky-sweet family excursion. And talk about cute. They're gazing so steadfastly into each other's eyes that they have yet to notice that their baby is sticking bark chips up his nose.

- ༄ **The "Busy" Executive.** Whoever said that taking care of a baby is hard work has obviously never learned to multitask. Because it's easy to watch a baby, manage a budgeting spreadsheet, and lead a conference call at the same time. (You may want to keep an eye on his kid while he "multitasks"—there's no reason to put a baby's health at risk because daddy has to check the stock market.)

Mommy & Me Classes

I'm a joiner. I like being part of groups and cliques and secret clubs that only the smart, savvy moms who know enough to Google "local mom's clubs" get permission to join. Yes, I'm that mom. So it probably doesn't surprise you that I asked Mr. Google about "Mommy & Me" classes before Joey was even born. And that he was less than four months old when he took his first trial class.

In the hour leading up to our first Mommy & Me class, I walked him through a series of warm-up exercises in order to warm up our vocal cords (*la-la-la-la-la-la-la-la-la*) and I have to admit I was slightly frustrated when his excitement levels at the prospect of not only getting out of the house, but also being able to join his peers for an hour of athleticism and music weren't quite on par with mine. But whatever. He probably just didn't know what to expect.

We arrived early and immediately assessed the scene. I spotted the type A supermommy right away, standing in front of the gate, gently stretching her daughter's arms to warm up her muscles (why didn't I think of *that*?) and the exhausted mom of triplets in the corner, trying desperately to herd her three crawling babies without looking desperate. I introduced Joey to the teacher, proudly explaining that he was only five months old, but I was enrolling him in the five-to-eight-month-old class, as he had shown advanced core strength for his age and was already sitting up. The important things, right?

Class began and I immediately knew that this was the place where Joey was going to thrive academically, physically, and emotionally. Sure, he was acting a bit cautious (okay, terrified) as we sang loudly about purple balloons and red trucks. And he wasn't really interested in the balls. But regardless, I could just tell that he was absorbing essential information and skills at an astonishing rate. I had to suppress some momentary panic about how I was going to manage to raise a genius child.

Now, it turns out that the other children in the class were brilliant as well. Each and every one of them sat there quietly while the instructor sang. And each and every one batted at the bubbles and squealed at the parachute. So, naturally, we parents of gifted children needed to band together to assure the proper growth and development of our prodigy children. At least that's what I told my husband when I tried to justify the seventy-five-dollars per-month tuition to keep taking the class.

There's a slight chance I got caught up in Gymboree fever. It was a chance to get out of the house, and in my cooped-up-with-only-a-baby-to-talk-to state, I admit that I was a little desperate for human interaction as well as something to do with my baby besides play with rattles. And Gymboree fit the mold perfectly. And Joey liked it—don't get me wrong—but undoubtedly, I liked it more than he did. And I learned more from it than he did.

So before you go dye your hair black in protest of moms like me who seem to think Mommy & Me classes are a pillar to a successful education, hear me out. I know deep down inside that these classes are totally unnecessary and slightly ridiculous. I know that my third baby, Will—who, by the way, has never stepped foot inside a baby gym—is just as smart as Joey, who was a Mommy & Me regular for the first three years of his life. I get that. But I also know that

Mommy & Me classes can be a lot of fun. So if it's something you want to do and can afford, I say go for it.

Finding Mommy-and-Me Activities in Your Town

I live in Austin, Texas, which is a rather large city that boasts some sort of baby-centric locale on nearly every corner. We have My Gym and Little Gym and Gymboree and Kindermusik and a million other options that meant I was not only able to pick and choose my mommy-and-me activities but also able to take about fifteen free trial classes before selecting my home base. Not only did this allow me to be selective in choosing mommy-and-me activities that fit my requirements (read: no out-loud singing in front of crowds), but it also kept Joey and me busy for several weeks before we had even spent a dime.

That said, if you live in the city, you probably have a plethora of mommy-and-me choices. But if you live way out in the sticks (that's what my six-year-old likes to call anyplace that's more than six minutes away from his school), you may have a hard time finding mommy-and-me activities. Here are a few ideas:

1. **The YMCA**. The Y offers all sorts of fun, kid-centric classes—and even if you're not a member, they are often fairly inexpensive. When Joey was a baby, I enrolled him in a great mommy-and-me swim class at the Y and we had all sorts of fun splashing and pretending to be motorboats.

2. **Churches**. I'm amazed at the ingenuity of some churches. There's a church in our neighborhood that offers a Bible heroes camp for kids ten and under every summer. Even the babies get involved in the fun by being given the opportunity to listen to the music, watch the games from the arms of their mommies, and more.

3. **Parks & rec**. There's a Leslie Knope in every town who is working behind the scenes to come up with fun activities for your kids. I heard about a baby foot-printing class at one of our parks awhile back. Parents could go and splotch their

babies' little tootsies in a pan of paint and create these ador-able keepsake footprint pictures. (The best part: the paint stays at the park, and never has the chance to end up on your carpet.)

4. **Stores**. Check out the bulletin boards of your local kids' stores to find all sorts of fun things to do. Home Depot, Michael's, Lowes, and Buy Buy Baby are all known for posting and even hosting fun (and sometimes free) workshops, classes, and more fun to-dos for babies and their parents.

Get Outta There!

Did you know that the amount of time you spend cooped up in your house has a direct correlation to the amount of time you spend whining about being cooped up in your house? Okay, so I'm totally making that up (I'm not one for statistics—who would've guessed?), but I can pretty much say with some level of certainty that you'll be a much happier, saner mom if you at least attempt to venture into the real world every once in a while. Even if it's just a quick trip to the grocery store to buy milk. Because I think we both know that attempting to drink coffee without milk is a surefire way to ruin a perfectly good day at home with baby. And there you have it, folks: sheer, mathematical proof that it's in everyone's best interest for you to leave the house. Today.

TWELVE

Solid Advice

Feeding Your Baby Real Food
(Cowritten by Registered Dietitian Alisa Dusan)

I just want to start out by saying that you modern moms have it so easy.

Back in the day when I had my first baby (way back in 2005), those little squeezie pouches full of baby food hadn't even been invented yet. We had to suffer through the inconvenience of spooning our baby's food out of—get this—a bowl. And as we slowly lifted spoonful after endless spoonful of strained peas into our babies' mouths, we dreamt of a day when mothers would be spared this incredible inconvenience.

But you guys, well, you have birthed your babies in the squeezie-pouch era! You have access to amazing new technology, like Baby Brezza baby food makers, spinach-and-pear blends that taste nothing like spinach and totally like pears, and—my personal favorite—spoons that screw onto said squeezie pouches and let food seep through. All while I had to walk uphill both ways to my pediatrician's office, carrying two babies and a bag full of frozen breast milk. Don't feel too sorry for me. I survived, and I'm tougher because of my pain.

Anyway, just so you don't think my information in this chapter is totally outdated, I want to assure you that I know the ins and outs of feeding in the squeezie-pouch era. My late addition, Will (not that I'm calling him a surprise or anything), was born in 2011 and thus has been raised on squeezies. I've tasted the glory of modern parenting. I know the difference between plain old jarred carrots and purple carrots-and-blueberries-with-antioxidants-and-Samba.

But just because I've done it doesn't make me an expert—so I recruited (okay, bribed) my sister, Alisa—you know, the registered dietitian who helped whip us into shape in the losing-the-baby-weight chapter—to help tell you exactly how and what you should be feeding your baby. And if you don't believe me (see: walked uphill to the pediatrician both ways in the snow), believe her. Here's our best solid-food starting advice.

When to Start Your Baby on Solid Foods

Now, the first thing you're probably wondering is how early you can get Junior into a high chair so you can snap some adorable pictures of him covered in sweet potatoes. Because that's what moms do. But let me just tell you from experience: the whole sweet potato thing really isn't all it's cracked up to be. Not only do the pictures rarely turn out as cute as you imagine them to be, but afterward you have to spend twenty minutes in the bathtub scrubbing caked-on sweet potatoes out of your baby's eyelashes.

As a general rule, your pediatrician will probably tell you to start solid foods sometime when your baby is between four and six months old. But since you asked my opinion (you did, didn't you?), I say skew more toward six months than four because starting solid foods awakens a time-sucking beast. Between food prep, actual feeding, and cleanup, you'll spend a good portion of your day just feeding (and cleaning) your baby. A portion of your day that could've been spent doing truly productive things, like stalking Jennifer Garner's Twitter feed.

There will come a point somewhere around six months (give or take a month or two) that you notice your baby taking swipes at your mashed potatoes every time you try to get them into your mouth. And at that point—provided he can also hold his head up steadily and sit in a somewhat upright position with support—it's probably time to start prepping your camera—and your bathtub—for the introduction to solid food.

Your Baby Feeding Plan

As you've probably figured out by now, I'm fairly type A. So when I start something new—especially something I've never done before—I want a plan. A plan that tells me exactly what to do and how to do it and gives me side notes and footnotes and anecdotes to account for every possible deviation from said plan. So for all of you type A moms like me, I've taken the liberty of twisting Alisa's arm until she said she'd write you a step-by-step plan on how to introduce solid foods for your baby.

Of course, before I lay out our plan, I do recognize that not all moms are type A like me. In fact, some of you are probably like my husband, who thought it was a good idea to just squirt some baby food into a bowl and feed it to my baby without writing up an hour-by-hour, color-coded feeding schedule. Who does that? But apparently some people do. And since I'm willing to admit that just because somebody does something differently than I would, it doesn't mean she's wrong (thanks, Mom!), I'm willing to also concede that you type B moms may feel slightly overwhelmed by our thoroughly researched and fully indexed baby feeding plan. So I made you a plan of your own. Because I'm nice like that.

The Type B Plan for Starting Solids

Step 1: Put whatever pureed baby food you have on hand into a bowl or cup.

Step 2: Spoon-food into your baby's mouth.

Step 3: Repeat whenever your baby is hungry.

Step 4: Skip reading the rest of this chapter and, instead, e-mail my husband to talk about how type A parents complicate even the simplest things.

The Type A Plan for Starting Solids

Step 1: Start with a single-grain, iron-fortified baby cereal (Alisa and I recommend oats because it's less constipating than rice or wheat) and mix it with breast milk or formula to make it runny. (For you exact-measurement types, try about four tablespoons of liquid for every tablespoon of cereal.) Feed this to baby once per day—not *instead of* breast milk or formula but *in addition* to it. Baby food is very similar to those super–low-calorie dinners you bought at the grocery store last week. Sure, they look delicious and filling, but even after devouring the entire plate in one bite, you're still hungry. Same goes for your baby's food. Until he's eating loads of the stuff, he should still be getting the majority of his calories from breast milk or formula.

Step 2: You'll know your baby is getting the hang of eating cereal when he stops gagging every time you spoon it into his mouth. At that point, start adding more of the grain and less of the milk so his little porridge gradually gets thicker and thicker. This may take a few days—or, if your baby is anything like my nephew Jacob, who threw up every time solid foods hit his lips, a few weeks. And that's okay. Some babies just need more time to adjust to the different textures in their mouths. (And by the way, if someone tells you that your baby has sensory integration issues because he's having trouble adjusting to solid foods, you have my permission to roll your eyes and ignore everything that person says from that point on. Because that's just ridiculous and totally unfounded. Ask your doctor if you don't believe me.)

Step 3: Once your baby is chowing down cereal like a champ, you can start adding other foods. Now, there are two strategies when it comes to introducing other foods. Strategy one involves giving your baby a fruit or veggie— say, pears—and then waiting three days before trying another food. That way, if you see signs of an allergy (diarrhea, vomiting, rash, wheezing, or a swollen face), you'll know exactly what food caused the allergy. Strategy two involves just giving your baby fruits and veggies willy-nilly, and if you see an allergic reaction, backing off all foods that you had fed your baby the three days prior. I'm sure you can guess which strategy I used.

(Side note: You may have been told to introduce veggies first so your kiddo doesn't develop a sweet tooth. But I've got bad news for you: your baby picked up his sweet tooth on day one when he got that first big swig of milk. If you want to introduce veggies first so you can tell all your friends that Junior's first and favorite food has always been broccoli, then be my guest. But it's probably not going to have any effect on his future love of green beans.)

Step 4: Offer a few slurps of water in a sippy cup at mealtime. This will not only serve to teach your baby how to drop his cup and scream, "Uh-oh!" the moment you sit down to eat, but also help him transition away from using bottles later. And just as a general rule, it's probably better to hold off on juice for as long as possible. Juice is like Diet Dr Pepper for babies. It's delicious and oh-so-refreshing, but before you know it, he'll be popping the top on six juice boxes a day and making midnight runs to the 7-11 to get a fix.

Step 5: Once your baby is slurping down a fair amount of strained carrots in each feeding, you can start to increase the number of meals you serve him each day. Maybe add a little smooshed peach breakfast to the mix one day or a butternut squash aperitif the next. If you want definite numbers (*sheesh*, you numbers people), a seven-month-old should probably be eating two meals a day and by eight months you should probably at least give him something for breakfast, lunch, and dinner. As you add more solid food, you can start to decrease breast milk or formula—but how much and how quickly is a question for your pediatrician.

Step 6: Somewhere around nine months old—once your baby can sit up on his own and is starting to get up onto his hands and knees—you can start introducing table food. This basically means you can start feeding your baby delicious snacks like Cheerios or star puffies. You can also start chopping up tiny pieces of whatever you're eating and letting your baby sample chicken enchilada bake or Pad Thai.

Making Your Own Baby Food

I'm sure a lot of you who are reading this (remember, the type B moms have already dropped this chapter and are off playing pat-a-cake with their babies) are thinking that you're going to make your own baby food. Like grind your own whole grains into baby cereals and boil, smoosh, and strain fresh organic fruits and veggies into fancy little homemade purees. And I hope you succeed as you turn your home into a one-stop baby-food-making shop. Really, I do.

But before you go out and buy a bushel of organic peaches, let me at least attempt to be a voice of reason. Because as wonderful and supermom-ish as it sounds to make all of your baby's food using all-organic ingredients and a heaping dose of love, I want to remind you that each batch of organic baby food you make means a lot of time spent in the kitchen slaving over a hot stove (or at least a sort-of-hot baby-food maker)—and unless you've mastered the art of slicing, dicing, peeling, and steaming with one arm, you'll probably have to do this while your baby is napping. Which means you're going to spend a lot of your could-have-been-Pinteresting time making baby food.

Now, before you label me as slacker-mom and start to disregard everything I say, I need to clarify that I haven't always taken the just-buy-it-and-save-yourself-some-time stance. Had I written this book six years ago, I would've probably included a whole chapter full of step-by-step instructions on how to puree baby food and included fifteen of my favorite recipes. But I have changed. (That may have something to do with the three kids running around my house.) And I now know that I'd rather spend eighty-nine cents on a squeezie pouch of smooshed bananas than spend eighty-nine hours making my own smooshed bananas.

All that said, if you're still gung ho about making homemade baby food (Seriously? Not even the Pinterest thing convinced you?), then I will go ahead and tell you that its not nearly as hard or as supermom-esque as I just made it seem. And Alisa just reminded me that, technically, it can be great for your baby because you'll know for a fact that no one snuck a few spoonfuls of Kool-Aid powder into your strained pears to make them more colorful. (Unless, of course, you have an older-sibling helper, in which case you can't be so sure.) That, and if you happen to puree whatever you're eating, your baby will get used to how you cook, which will really come in handy in four years when he decides that the head chef at McDonald's has more culinary skills than you do.

But I digress. Here are the steps to making your own baby food:

Step 1: Cook it. I found that the fastest way to cook produce for baby food was to steam it in a stovetop steamer. You just peel, core, and dice the peaches or apples or whatever, steam for a few minutes until they are soft, and then set them aside to cool. You can also try baking (which works great for apples and sweet potatoes) or boiling (for things like butternut squash and chicken).

Step 2: Blend it. Once the food is cooked and cooled, you can pop it in the blender or food processor to puree. If it's too thick, you can add a bit of breast milk, formula, or water to thin it out.

Step 3: Store it. If you're feeling really ambitious and you want to make a big batch of food all at once, just pour any food that your baby won't eat in the first three or four days into an ice cube tray. When it's frozen, pop out the cubes and store them in the freezer in a gallon-size Ziploc bag.

Step 4: Eat it. Grab a couple of cubes and defrost them either in the fridge or in a bowl of hot water. Eat and enjoy.

One last disclaimer before we move on—this one from my totally type B husband who happens to be reading over my shoulder and shaking his head while I write this. He says that, technically, you could skip the steps above and make your own baby food simply by mashing up a ripe banana or avocado with your fork and calling it good. And, technically, he's right. But I'm not one for technicalities, and I say if you're going to go as far as making your baby's food from scratch, then you may as well go all out and use the type A method when you do it.

Finger Foods

You'll know it's time to start feeding Lil' Mr. Grabby Pants finger foods because he'll start, well, grabbing everything. And, at that point, you'll quickly realize that the only thing you're doing by force-feeding him squeezie pouches (or, if you're one of *those* moms, homemade organic food cubes) is helping him paint the wall a beautiful shade of sweet-potato orange. This usually happens at about nine months of age—and I have to say that each time my kids hit this stage, I felt an acute sense of relief when I realized I could toss a few small chunks on the high chair tray and then sit back and drink my coffee without having to make airplane sounds with a baby spoon.

The key to being successful as you introduce your baby to finger foods is to chop every morsel into the teeniest, tiniest pieces ever. Blueberries? They get cut into quarters. Grapes? Sixteenths. I'll concede that it's okay to leave Cheerios whole, but that doesn't mean I haven't ever tried breaking them in half before giving them to my babies. Just to be on the safe side.

Aside from the teeny-tiny piece rule, the sky is pretty much the limit when it comes to finger food. You can go ahead and give your baby whatever you have on hand—and provided it's not super spicy, you're probably safe. Here are some of Alisa's best first finger-food suggestions:

- Crunchy toast cut up into tiny pieces
- Itsy pieces of soft fruit, like bananas, mango, soft pears, and watermelon
- Small, well-cooked pasta
- Chopped hard-boiled egg or scrambled eggs
- Very small chunks of soft cheese
- Small, chopped, well-cooked pieces of veggies, like asparagus, green beans, or broccoli
- Pea-sized pieces of cooked chicken, steak, or fish

Starting Healthy from the Get-Go

My niece Haddie's first food was a small bite of a doughnut that her grandma snuck her when she was three months old. Needless to say, my sister wasn't too happy about that. But Haddie actually came through what we now have deemed "the Krispy Kreme incident" unscathed. She even eats the occasional fruit or veggie without too much protesting.

All that said, what you feed your baby today will lay the foundation for healthy lifelong eating habits. So take a moment now to consider the ramifications of how the food choices you make today will change your baby's life forever—and then move on to feeling annoyed with me for trying to pass comments like that one off as inspirational, when in truth you don't need motivation right now. What you need is for someone to tell you what to do to build that healthy foundation.

Insert deep breath here. You're smart enough to know that fruits and veggies and lean proteins are healthy—and Twizzlers and Doritos chased down with Mountain Dew are not. And I'm guessing you even know that by introducing your kids to a variety of healthy foods now, you'll at least have a jump start on dealing with those quintessential toddler cheese-and-candy-only food jags. I'm here to help. Of course, my help probably means next to nothing since I'm hardly a food expert, but Alisa's here to help too, and here's how she suggests you give your baby the best healthy-eating start you can.

- **Choose lots of colors** . . . and I'm not talking about the kinds of colors in Froot Loops. Instead, look for colorful produce—because deep, dark colors often indicate those fruits and veggies are loaded with nutrients. The more different colors you feed your baby, the more different nutrients they'll be getting.
- **Kick up the flavor.** Alisa was telling me about a client she had who hired her to help figure out foods that her two picky kids would eat. When Alisa showed up at her house, she knew right away what was up: Mom wasn't adding any flavor to the kids' food. Early exposure to lots of different flavors—think, cinnamon, curry, fresh herbs—may actually

help your child be less picky later on. And if you really think about it, would you rather eat bland and flavorless broiled fish and mushy peas or that fantastic cilantro-baked halibut that your friends raved about last summer?

⌒ **Embrace healthy fats**. Take everything you've ever learned about low-fat eating and just forget about it. Not because it's a good idea to go load up on french fries and deep-fried ice cream, but simply because human beings need some good fats to stay healthy. And this is especially true for babies. So load your baby's diet with the healthy fats that come from foods like avocado, olive oil, and fish, and don't be scared of foods like full-fat yogurt and whole milk.

Food Allergies

Back when Joey was born (remember, this was pre–squeezie-pouch era), my pediatrician told me I needed to avoid all commonly allergenic foods for the first couple of years of his life in order to decrease his risk of developing a food allergy. So, since I'm a rule follower to the core, I followed that rule to the letter. Joey did not taste wheat, eggs, milk, soy, fish, berries, nuts, or citrus before his first birthday. If my doctor hadn't shown me the new research—research that debunked the whole avoid-allergenic-foods strategy—I would've kept Joey away from Reese's Peanut Butter Cups until he went to college. Imagine, a childhood without Reese's. What was I thinking?

But, thankfully for Joey (and all the kids in the squeezie-pouch generation), most pediatricians aren't recommending delayed exposure to allergens anymore because there's really no evidence that it does anything to prevent food allergies. (Seriously, call your pediatrician and ask . . . I won't say I told you so.) This may freak you type A rule followers out, but it's perfectly okay to feed your baby most foods—including common allergens, like peanuts, eggs, and dairy—before his first birthday. That means scrambled eggs for breakfast, yogurt for lunch, and (gasp!) fish for dinner is A-OK.

If you're really wanting to play it safe, you can introduce highly allergic foods at home, where you have Benadryl on hand and can watch your baby for a few hours afterward. But the bottom line is this: if your kid is allergic to peanuts, your kid is allergic to peanuts. And delaying exposure won't prevent a reaction. And truth be told, if your kid is allergic to peanuts, you probably want to know sooner rather than later.

Of course, there are a few exceptions to these new rules. You should talk to your doctor before trying highly allergenic foods if you have a strong family history of food allergies or asthma or if your baby shows any signs of allergy, like eczema. And of course, call your doctor ASAP or head to the ER if you think your kiddo might be having an allergic reaction.

Baby Food No-No's

I'm really always crimping your Christian mama style, aren't I? I mean, I just told you that your baby can pretty much feast on anything he wants, and now I'm going to turn around and poo-poo that by giving you a list of no-nos. But, if it helps, it's not really a list. It's just a few tiny things:

- **Honey and corn syrup** can contain spores that can cause a very dangerous disease called infant botulism. It's best to keep your baby away from that PB & honey sandwich until he's at least one.
- **Citrus fruits, corn, and berries** can cause horrible diaper rash in some babies, so if you notice a rash, you may want to cut those foods out.
- **Cow's milk** doesn't contain everything your baby needs to

grow and develop, so it's best to stick with breast milk or formula until after his first birthday.

- ❧ And last, but certainly not least, there are many foods that are **choking hazards**. Cut grapes, hot dogs, raw carrots, nuts, and tough chunks of meat into teeny-tiny pieces and avoid hard candy and popcorn until your baby is old enough to chew well. You also may want to watch out for big globs of peanut butter. (Don't worry, you can still grab spoonfuls out of the jar; just don't feed them to your baby.)

The Christian Mama's Mini Guide to Mealtime

Unless you have a regular Mensa genius on your hand—in which case you probably should be researching college admission requirements for two-year-olds instead of reading this book—your baby probably isn't contributing much to the dinnertime conversation. Yet. But setting the stage for great family meals starts now—right when your baby is learning what exactly eating and mealtime is. Show your baby just how fun it is to sit down for another home-cooked meal of macaroni and cheese (from the box, of course) with these simple family-mealtime tips.

- ❧ **Pray before you eat.** Before my niece Greta had even graduated to finger foods, she would sit down in her high chair and immediately bow her head and fold her hands. She had learned early that before you eat, you pray. And, aside from being about the cutest thing ever, she got in the habit of thanking God for her food from early on.
- ❧ **Embrace the mess.** Don't spend your entire dinner trying to keep everything spic-and-span. (That's why you got a dog, isn't it?) So take some simple steps (read: protect everything with a fine layer of protective plastic) to ensure that you can enjoy dinner without stressing about the mess.

- **Avoid power struggles**. Nothing can kill a fun family dinner faster than a good ole power struggle. If your baby doesn't want to eat a new food after trying a bite or two, don't stress about it or force it; just move on and try again the next day. And the next. And the next (repetition is the key).
- **Use the time to connect**. If your squawking ten-month-old seems to think that throwing sweet potatoes is more fun than talking politics, he may be onto something. But the rest of the time, you should try to engage your baby in the dinnertime conversation. Model what family mealtime is all about from day one. Put your cell phones to silent (yep, that means you too) and talk to each other. About something other than the sweet potatoes all over the dining room hutch (see "Embrace the mess" above).

10 Reasons Moms in the Squeezie Pouch Generation Have It Easy

1. Purple carrot stains blend in with the natural colors in clothing more often than orange carrot stains do.
2. Your kid can't say, "Uh-oh!" and drop his spoon on the floor if his spoon is screwed onto his food.
3. Organic fruits and vegetables are available outside of the farmers' market.
4. Two words: Puffy stars.
5. Three words: Baby Mum-Mums.
6. Even fancy-schmancy restaurants have high chairs these days. And caviar on the kids' menu.
7. Generation Squeezie moms can feed their babies quickly and efficiently in shopping carts, car seats, and subway cars. Notice I didn't say cleanly.
8. Even bibs have sleeves now.
9. Your baby can now ingest designer grains, like Samba and

quinoa. Because his diet was so limited when he only had access to wheat, oats, and rice.

10. Your baby eats more antioxidants in a day than you have in your entire lifetime.

THIRTEEN

Taking Care of You, You, You

Finding Time for You When the Baby Is Crying, "Me, Me, Me!"

Have you ever been *ovxausted*? Wait, no? Maybe you just don't know what *ovxausted* is. It's that new-mom state of foggy confusion where you feel so *overwhelmed* and so utterly *exhausted* that the only thing that's going to help you regain your sanity is a triple white chocolate mocha with whipped cream and a couple of hours crashed out on the couch. (Not in that order, of course.) So I might have made the word *ovxausted* up (I do that sometimes), but it's only because previously, there was no word in the English language to describe how new moms feel at the end of a long day. A day when their baby has slept for a grand total of twelve minutes. In the past twenty-four hours.

My friend Donnine told me that when her daughter was tiny, she was so *ovxausted* from trying to figure out breast-feeding that she inadvertently flashed an entire pizza restaurant full of people. She had been in the car, trying to feed her two-week-old daughter, and after ten frustrating minutes of trying to figure out a latch, she grabbed her baby and headed inside to get her husband. Except, in her state of *ovxaustion*, she forgot one little thing—to refasten her nursing bra and close her shirt. So, she climbed out of the car and tossed her diaper bag over her shoulder with all of the Christian mama style she could muster and headed inside. Only to glance down right as she walked into the restaurant and notice that, well, she wasn't exactly pulling off that look.

We've all been there. Okay, so we haven't all been there, there. (Sorry, Donnine.) But every new mom has been *ovxausted*. And in desperate need of a good old-fashioned time-out.

10 Ways You Know You're Ovxausted

1. You catch yourself pouring coffee creamer in the water reservoir of the coffee pot. Or worse, you don't catch yourself pouring cream into the water reservoir of the coffee pot but notice a few days later that the water in your coffee pot looks awfully creamy. And smells weird.
2. You can't remember the last time you wore clean clothes. Or matching socks.
3. If you were given a choice between an eight o'clock bedtime or an eight o'clock hot date with your hubby, you'd choose bedtime. Hands down.
4. Your status update on Facebook says, "Dear baby, if you would just start sleeping a bit more, Mommy would be a lot more fun at the playground" . . . and you're starting to get a bit annoyed that your baby hasn't "liked" it.
5. You proudly place a PB&J (without crusts) in front of your husband when he walks in the door from work and then go on to explain to him the incredible effort that went into making him "a decent dinner."

6. You do cry over spilled milk. And spilled laundry baskets. And spilled Cheerios.
7. You catch yourself watching singing bunny videos on YouTube.
8. You really can't see why it's that big of a deal for your baby to use your iPhone as a teething toy. Isn't that what the OtterBox is for?
9. The laundry is stacked so high on your bed that there's no room on your bed to lie down. So you just rest on the floor. The kitchen floor.
10. You ran out of coffee so you just munched on chocolate-covered espresso beans all day. And you feel just fine. Shaky, but fine.

Of course, part of being a mom is that you have to press through, even if you're so completely *ovxausted* that you've done all ten of the things on that list . . . in the last twenty minutes. But that doesn't mean you can check out and hop in a car and drive to Napa (something my husband and I once did when we were young and childless and didn't know that spending sixteen hours in a car on a Friday when you had to be back at work on a Monday is a very bad idea). You can, however, give yourself the rest, rejuvenation, and time you need so that in spite of everything, you can be the best mom you can be.

Taking a Time-Out

Pretty much the best thing you can do for yourself when you're *ovxausted* is to find a way to take a time-out. A little breather from parenting, if you will. I remember a time when Joey was about four months old when I was *ovxausted*. He hadn't quite gotten the hang of sleeping through the night so I was up at all hours feeding and rocking him. To top that off, my husband had gone back to work and was dealing with crazy work deadlines and extra hours, so I was feeling alone, overwhelmed, and in need of a break.

Now, get this: My sweet husband noticed that I needed some downtime—the sob session over the fact that I couldn't find my orange workout shorts may have clued him in—and planned this elaborate, long mommy time-out day just for me. He got up and showered, shaved, and then kissed me good-bye per his normal get-ready-for-work routine. But he was just being tricky. Because twenty minutes later, he was back, with a latte and a muffin from my favorite coffee shop in hand. He handed me my breakfast and then explained that he had a whole elaborate mommy-needs-a-time-out-day plan for me that included a massage, a manicure, lunch out, and—best of all—time to lie on the couch and read a novel without anybody slobbering on the pages. Pure bliss.

I'm going to pause for a second so you can run and grab a high-lighter for the above paragraph. Then you can leave this book open on your hubby's nightstand and pray that he reads said paragraph and it sparks an idea that perhaps he, too, should plan a daylong mom-stravaganza for you. Or you could just tell him that it's what you want.

Anyway, while I was away getting my massage, I started think-ing about how if I just had a mommy time-out day planned for one day every week, I would be not only a better mom but a sassier and sexier wife as well. I mean, how hard can life be if you have a mas-sage and mani-pedi on the schedule? I tried later to convince my husband of this fact, and he agreed wholeheartedly until he real-ized that I was somewhat serious and that he didn't have the time nor money to make it happen. Whatever. I said I was only somewhat serious.

After all that, I realized that while an occasional all-out time-out is a great thing—and something all husbands should do for their hardworking wives from time to time—by building mini mommy time-outs into my days, I could be proactive in saving my sanity and my attitude—and even my marriage.

Time-Out for Mom

"May the God of hope fill you with all joy and peace as you trust in him, so that you may overflow with hope by the power of the Holy Spirit." (Romans 15:13)

My God of hope, thank You for filling me with joy and peace even when I am feeling overwhelmed and exhausted. My cup overflows with You. I pray that You will come stand beside me now and help me feel refreshed and ready to face whatever is in store for the day. Amen.

The Mommy Guilts

I used to tell myself that I didn't need time-outs from my kids because I work. I had this crazy idea that because I chose to work, I needed to spend every waking moment that I wasn't working watching my kids. I went even further and thought about how the five minutes I took each day to shower alone was certainly enough to give me the wind-down time I needed. What else did I expect? Isn't sacrificing every moment of free time that you could possibly have an expectation that comes with parenthood?

I now know that all of those crazy thoughts and ideas were the result of a very prevalent condition called the Mommy Guilts. And I had it bad. I felt guilty for letting someone else watch my kids so I could work. I felt guilty that I only worked part-time so I could be with my kids and didn't make as much money for the family as I would with a full-time job. And every time I even thought about work or kids or the fact that it had been six months since I'd taken a bubble bath, I'd melt into a spiral of guilt that was only cured by a Dove chocolate binge.

Before I go on, I want to clarify that the Mommy Guilts aren't exclusive to working moms. The Mommy Guilts are prevalent with all types of moms. Working moms feel guilty that they work. Stay-at-home moms feel guilty that they don't contribute to the household income. Work-from-home moms feel guilty that they are caught between two worlds and often unable to focus wholly on either. I guess the only moms who escape the Mommy Guilts are those who have forty-eight hours in every day—twenty-four with which to work and twenty-four with which to focus on their kids. Those moms have it so easy. But, the rest of us, we feel guilty.

But—and here's where I get all preachy at you—there is no reason to feel guilty! I have no doubt that you have prayerfully made the decisions you have made for your family. And those decisions are the decisions that work for you. There is no condemnation in Christ! And there is no reason to feel guilty for the choices you've made— whether they are to work, to stay home, or to do some combination of the two. And what's more, there is no reason to let the Mommy Guilts stand in the way of you taking the time you need to overcome ovxaustion. Because when you're ovxausted, you're never going to be the mom, the wife, the worker, or the woman God called you to be. So kick the guilt—and your ovxaustion—to the curb. Let's take a time-out.

A Spiritual Time-Out

I'm certainly not the first person to tell you that you have to be intentional in finding time for God when you're a mom. Because I think finding time to grow spiritually is one of the most difficult issues moms face. Before I had kids, I was actually pretty good about having a regular quiet time. My work schedule was predictable, so I could get up at the same time every day, make a cup of coffee, and then spend time reading the Bible and praying. Once I got into the habit, I rarely missed a day.

But then I had Joey. And you already know that baby sleep schedules are unpredictable. And you can already guess that once Joey was born, setting my alarm at the same time every day to have a quiet time worked about as well as the *Your Baby Can Do Algebra* CD my friend gave me (read: not at all).

But just because something is hard doesn't mean you shouldn't do it. (You may want to go grab that highlighter again and highlight that last sentence.) I know that sounds like something your mom would say, but your mom is pretty darn smart. And having a spiritual time-out every day is really important for your spiritual health. Here are some tricks that helped me find the time—and the energy— to make time for God every day.

1. **Schedule a time for quiet time**. First thing in the morning probably won't work unless your baby has somehow managed to adopt the sleeping patterns of a college freshman—but that doesn't mean there aren't other predictable times to schedule your quiet time every day. For me, I did my Bible-and-prayer time right after I put my son down for his morning nap. You could also schedule quiet time right before bed or during your baby's bath time (if your husband is on bath duty, of course).

2. **Get a journal**. I'm a writer. So to say that the idea of writing my thoughts down in a little notebook to keep for posterity appeals to me is a slight understatement. It's about my favorite thing ever. But even if you're not an obsessive documentarian like I am, having a journal where you can write down your prayers, your spiritual insights, and favorite verses can help you stay on track during quiet time (an essential when you're running on two hours of sleep). Plus, it's really fun to go back and reread past journal entries and realize just how many prayers God has answered.

3. **Use a guide**. There's some amazing Christian literature and devotionals that can help you connect with God on a deeper level during your quiet time. The book I'm reading right now, *Mama Needs a Time-Out* (by Heather Riggleman), has these

great daily devotions about how you can find God in the midst of motherhood. Another resource I love is a book I worked on with my friend Kathi Lipp. It's titled *Praying God's Word for Your Life,* and it guides you on how to use Scripture to pray for your kids, your relationships, your anxieties, and every other area of your life.

4. **Pray continuously.** There is no reason to box prayer time into a small, thirty-minute window in your day. (That's like boxing coffee time into the morning hours.) I've been trying to get into the habit of praying throughout my day, whenever a thought pops into my mind. So, as I make breakfast, I'm thanking God for His incredible provision. As I play with my kids, I'm pouring out my heart for their futures in Christ.

5. **Listen to music.** I've found that one of the best ways to calm myself down when I'm emotionally and spiritually ovxausted is to take Dan Zanes off of my iPod playlist (I love him, but there are days when I just can't hear anything else about trains) and pop in some amazing praise and worship music. Nothing like a little Jesus Culture or David Crowder to calm my spirit . . . and my nerves.

6. **Take mini time-outs.** Just because it's not your official quiet time doesn't mean you can't spend a few minutes reading a short devotion or a few verses from Scripture whenever and wherever you can steal a few minutes alone.

. . . .

SIDEBAR:

I have a list of calming scriptures on my fridge that I refer to whenever I need a quick pick-me-up. Here's what's on my list:

↪ Isaiah 40:31: "But those who hope in the LORD will renew their strength. They will soar on wings like eagles; they will run and not grow weary, they will walk and not be faint."

- Psalm 37:23–24: "The LORD makes firm the steps of the one who delights in him; though he may stumble, he will not fall, for the LORD upholds him with his hand."
- Jeremiah 29:11: "'For I know the plans I have for you,'" declares the LORD, 'plans to prosper you and not to harm you, plans to give you hope and a future.'"
- Ephesians 2:10: "For we are God's handiwork, created in Christ Jesus to do good works, which God prepared in advance for us to do."
- Psalm 112
- Proverbs 3:5–6: "Trust in the LORD with all your heart and lean not on your own understanding; in all your ways submit to him, and he will make your paths straight."
- Psalm 31
- 1 Thessalonians 5:17–18: "Pray continually, give thanks in all circumstances; for this is God's will for you in Christ Jesus."

A Working Mommy Time-Out

I told my husband a few months ago that if he would just quit his job, my life would be a lot easier. I'd have someone to help me watch the baby and pick the big kids up from school. I'd never have to scramble to find someone to watch the kids if I had an appointment. And I'd never have to juggle making dinner with three hungry and tired kids underfoot while my husband sat in yet another work meeting. But he didn't think that was a very good idea. Apparently he thinks things like paying the mortgage and buying groceries are important. So he's keeping his job. And I'm going to have to figure out how to survive without access to 24/7 on-call child care. Some guys can be so demanding, can't they?

I guess I can see my husband's point. But that doesn't mean I didn't have a small mourning period as my dreams came crashing down around my feet. Now that I've recovered, I do realize that the vast majority of moms are in my same boat—feeling a bit ovxausted and overwhelmed but unable to just pass their babies off to someone else and go for a spa day. But you can take care of your baby and yourself at the same time. Here are a few mommy-and-me breaks that both you and your baby will enjoy.

20 Mommy-and-Me Mini-Breaks

1. Go see a movie. Many theaters now offer baby days, where you can bring your baby and catch your favorite flick with other baby mamas.
2. Take your baby to the park and push him in the baby swing.
3. Thumb through a magazine while your baby plays on a blanket or in his ExerSaucer.
4. Make a pot of tea and sip it while your baby lounges next to you. If you're up to it, read him some board books.
5. Go to the pet store and let your baby look at the hamsters, birds, and fish.
6. Dress yourselves up and go get your photos taken at JC Penney or Picture People. Even if you only buy one shot, you'll have a lot of fun seeing all the cute expressions your baby makes.
7. Put your baby in a stroller and go window-shopping at the mall.
8. Share a scone at your favorite coffee shop. (The latte, well, that's only for you.)
9. Get outside. Calm down in the fresh air, and soak up some vitamin D.
10. Go to Target and give yourself permission to not even go near the baby section. Unless you want to, of course.
11. Take your baby to the Inflatable Palace. Most of the time, kids under one are free, and there are great play areas where moms of the sub-toddler set congregate.
12. Turn up the iPod and dance around the room with your baby in your arms.

13. Go on a drive to look at the spring wildflowers or the fall colors or the Christmas lights.
14. Go get fro-yo.
15. My friend Jessica sends out an "SOS" code to her girlfriends. They know that means to grab their babies and a box of cookies and head over to her house *stat*. Because misery turns into a party when there's company.
16. Get down on the floor—and out of the view of the piles of dishes in the sink—and spend some time just being with your baby.
17. Watch *American Idol*. (Hint: You can skirt the whole babies-shouldn't-watch-TV-until-they-are-twenty-seven issue by turning him backward so he can just hear the music. Not that I've ever done that.)
18. Skype with Grandma.
19. Skype with your best friend, who also has a baby, so you can be reassured that your crazy-messy-wild house is actually a crazy-messy-normal house.
20. Take up a mommy-and-me hobby. Try bird-watching (ie, walking around the neighborhood and pointing out birdies) or massage (ie, rubbing your baby's tootsies until he falls asleep).

Taking a Break Just for You, You, You

I used to view nap time as time to check things off of my to-do list. So I'd tuck my baby into bed and instantly morph into a domestic diva, dashing bleary-eyed from folding laundry to doing dishes to mopping the floor. And the entire time I'd cheer myself on by thinking about the fact that if I didn't get the laundry folded and put away or the dishes washed and loaded, I'd be an utter failure to myself, my baby, and my husband to boot. I'm not hard on myself at all.

It took a stern talking-to from my husband—well, that and my infamous packet-of-bubble-gum-in-the-washing-machine incident—to convince me that it was okay to take a few minutes off in the course of each day for a little me time. And while, yes, the laundry has to be folded by someone (and if your household runs anything like mine does, that someone is not going to be your husband), it can be folded later. Because I'm giving you my official permission to take a little break.

20 Just-for-Mom Mini-Breaks

1. Pin recipes on Pinterest that you know you'll never be able to make (read: chocolate coconut mini-soufflés) but look delicious anyway.
2. Watch *Parenthood* reruns.
3. Start that novel that you've been scheming in your head since you were in the fourth grade. So what if you only have time to write two pages before your baby wakes up? Or before he turns ten?
4. Call your childhood best friend and catch up.
5. Look at pictures of your childhood best friend's kids on Facebook and comment on how much they look exactly like she did when she was a kid.
6. Plan your next vacation.
7. Read a novel.
8. Redecorate your bedroom. In your head, at least.
9. Watch *Hoarders*. Then give yourself a pat on the back for being such a great housekeeper.
10. Clean out your junk drawer. (Yes, that's therapeutic to some people. Not to me, but I swear, there are ladies out there who like stuff like that.)
11. Text your husband flirty messages.
12. Shop for baby clothes online, even if you don't buy anything.
13. Read the latest on your favorite blogs.
14. See how many likes you can get in twenty minutes on your Facebook status.

15. Take a shower. And stay in there long enough to shave your legs and rinse out the conditioner.
16. Bust out *Cooking Light* and plan the dinner menu that you would make if you (a) felt like cooking, and (b) weren't terrified of venturing into the grocery store with your baby to buy ingredients.
17. Cook yourself a gourmet lunch—grilled cheese anyone?—and savor every last bite.
18. Take a bubble bath, and stay in until the water gets cold.
19. Do ab exercises. There's nothing like doing a set of twenty sit-ups to make you realize that you feel pretty darn good about the state of your abs. Just the way they are.
20. Start a new hobby. Try knitting, bird-watching, or painting. Or Facebooking.

FOURTEEN

Baby Weight Boot Camp

*Losing the Baby Weight . . .
Eventually*

had no problem accepting the fact that I was going to gain a little weight (okay, a lot) when I was pregnant. I just chalked it up to the fact that my babies needed a lot (and I mean a *lot*) of cheese and crackers to grow and thrive. But that all went out the window the second I popped those babies out. I was on a mission. I wanted my pre-preggo body back, and I was going to do anything and everything to make that happen. Well, anything and everything that didn't involve time at the gym with a Jillian Michaels look-alike or a quinoa-and-fava-bean diet. That's just insane.

Still, I had visions of size 8 skinny jeans dancing through my head before my baby's two-week checkup. I was sick of the water weight, sick of the stretch marks, sick of not being able to hoist my husband's sweats over my thighs. I was sick of being fat. So

I did what any six-week postpartum mom with three kids would do after a long and difficult pregnancy—I signed up to run a half marathon, and I convinced Alisa, my former Division I athlete sister, to run it with me.

Seeing as how I have spent my entire life believing that a thirty-minute kickboxing class at the gym is enough exercise to support my chocolate-chip-cookie habit, this was definitely out of character for me. And when I collapsed on the field, hyperventilating after our first mile-and-a-quarter training run—a training run that involved a lot more walking than running, mind you—I was ready to quit and go back to my comfy spot on the couch.

But Alisa was a regular drill sergeant (a drill sergeant who let me take a break to walk whenever I needed it and placed bottles of Gatorade in convenient spots along our training route) who convinced me to keep running, keep training. One and a quarter miles turned into two, and two into four. Four months later I could easily go eight or nine miles alternating running and walking. I was training hard. For a half marathon.

Looking back, I'm really glad I did it. Not because it was always fun (you can go ahead and take my word for it that running is hardly ever fun), but because it was a great motivator for me to get back into shape. The half marathon helped me do a lot of really cool and fantastic things—get into great shape, eat healthier, and even get a much-needed break from my babies. But there was one thing it didn't do, and that was help me lose all the baby weight.

I have a theory that my body purposefully holds on to that extra weight for the first nine or ten months after pregnancy as a punishment for everything I put it through during pregnancy. That's not a proven fact, but it sure makes sense to me. And I'm telling you all of this completely discouraging information so you won't make the same mistake I did and go out and do a bunch of exercise for no reason at all. I'm kidding—I want to remind you that there's a lot more to being healthy than just losing weight. And if you're eating right and exercising, the baby weight will (eventually) come off.

I eventually did lose the baby weight and I did finish that half marathon. But not in that order. The half marathon was in October; I finally reached my pre-pregnancy weight in April. And while you may be one of those rare women who manages to slip into your pre-preg jeans before you even consider buying a couple of "in-between" pairs, there's also a chance that you're a normal woman like me—a woman who owns "in-between" jeans in about seven different sizes.

Just to make sure you get the help you need to get healthy, I'm sharing my own personal drill sergeant (my sister, Alisa, the registered dietitian, not Heidi Klum's trainer) with you, free of charge. She's going to tell you how to lose the weight by eating right the healthy way—without having to do crazy things like drink spinach smoothies and pretend they taste good. So, it's boot camp time. Let's start losing that baby weight.

Your Warm-Up

Not to be all too-cool-for-school (or in this case, too-cool-for-boot-camp) on you, but when I was on my must-lose-the-baby-weight rampage, I couldn't have cared less about all the reasons why I should've been patient to start losing the baby weight. Sure, my body needed time and energy to heal, and yes, dieting and exercising too soon can cause exhaustion and mood swings, and yada yada yada. But I was already tired. And those mood swings had nothing to do with the fact that I was trying to lose the baby weight too fast.

I don't have to tell you that I had the wrong attitude. The truth is that if you jump on the must-shed-pounds bandwagon too quickly, you're going to do more harm than good. Patience right now is important not only for your sanity (which may have been my problem) but also for your health and for the health of your baby. According to Mr. Google, limiting calories too soon can rob your body of the energy it needs to recover from pregnancy and can even affect your milk supply. And Mr. Google never lies.

Plus, I read this really horrible story online about how rapid weight loss in a nursing mom can cause your body to release toxins that are stored in your fat, and those toxins can end up in your breast milk. Yikes! If that's not motivation enough for you to skip that crazy zucchini-only super cleanse, then the fact that zucchini tastes mushy and bitter even at its best should seal the deal for you.

So there you have it: it's a bad idea to try to lose your baby weight too quickly. Instead you should first talk to your doctor about the right timing to start a weight-loss and exercise program, and then second, patiently implement said program without going overboard or eating too much zucchini. Because slow and steady wins the weight-loss race. Or something like that.

Eating to Lose the Baby Weight

Alisa says that when she's working with postpartum moms, she recommends that her moms lose about a pound and a half each week. She says this rate provides steady and noticeable weight loss, but doesn't affect a nursing mom's milk supply and doesn't make them feel that they have to deprive themselves of any food that tastes good. Of course, I'm sure that most of you are reading this and saying, "Great! I'd love to lose a pound and a half this week! But how?"

To help you out, Alisa put together some super-simple but super-helpful eating tips that will help make this concrete for even the most type A, calorie-crunching mamas out there, but will also satisfy you free-flowing eaters who just want to go with the flow and still lose the baby weight. Here's what she has to say.

> **Cut 500 calories**. To lose about 1.5 pounds per week, you'll need to cut about 500 calories per day out of your diet. You can do this simply (and unmathematically) by focusing on eating healthy foods like fruits, vegetables, whole grains, and lean meats, which, by default, will mean you'll eat less

calories than if you were munching on Doritos all day. Another option for you number-loving mamas is to keep track of your calories online or by using an app like My Fitness Pal. Most women need 1,500–2,200 calories per day to stay healthy. Nursing women need 2,000–2,700 calories a day on average. So track the calories you eat, and as long as you stay within the healthy ranges above, see how many calories you can cut from your diet.

- **Don't skip meals.** It's super tempting to skip a meal here or there—who needs more than coffee for breakfast anyway?—to help with weight loss. The problem is that this always backfires. Alisa explained to me that when you skip a meal, you actually set yourself up to overeat at the next meal. And let's just be honest: when you skip breakfast, you're totally grumpy by ten o'clock, and the only thing that's going to cure your mood is a snack. Or a big bowl of ice cream.

- **Think variety.** I think we all can admit that any limiting diet—whether it's the grapefruit-and-celery diet or the cookie diet—is, well, limiting. Not only does your body need a variety of vitamins and minerals to stay healthy, but you need a variety of flavors to keep yourself from going on a brownie binge. And Alisa admits that this advice may go against a lot of the trendy diet advice out there right now, but cutting an entire food group—whether it's grains or fats or meats—from your diet can often be more destructive than helpful. Sure, there are rare people who have serious food allergies to things like gluten or dairy—but the vast majority of the population would be healthiest if they strove to eat a diet that included a vast variety of foods eaten in sensible proportions without seriously limiting any one food group or ingredient.

- **Watch what you drink.** Drinks like soda, juice, and double mocha frappés with whipped cream add a lot of calories without much nutrition. Drinking water (and *lots* of it) is your best bet for hydrating. And staying well hydrated can make you feel less hungry. As a general rule, if your pee is clear or light in color, then you're doing a good job with your water intake.

∽ **Choose good fats.** Remember back in the day when as long as you were eating something fat-free, it was healthy? I remember buying a bag of sugar-coated gummy bears and thinking about how healthy I was eating because the package said "fat-free." Of course, at that time, I wouldn't have dared touch something crazy-fatty like an avocado. Anyway, thank goodness that research has proven that movement false. (I do love some guacamole.) The consensus among dietitians and those-who-know now is that while saturated fats should be limited to keep your heart healthy, healthy fats that you find in foods such as avocadoes, canola and olive oil, nuts, olives, and fish are not only really healthy for you, but if you're breast-feeding, super important for your baby's brain development. And if I can do something to ensure that my baby will get a full ride to college instead of me having to scrape together twenty grand to pay tuition, I'm going to do it.

Exercising to Lose the Baby Weight

Not to burst your I-can-eat-as-much-guacamole-as-I-want bubble, but I have a little bit of bad news for you. Mr. Google says that if you want to lose the baby weight and keep it off, you're also going to have to get a little sporty. And I know Mr. Google's information can be a bit untrustworthy from time to time, but in this case, I'm finding that most experts seem to agree. In fact, one doctor I talked to said that if you try to lose weight through dieting alone, you risk losing muscle mass instead of the fat you're really trying to lose. I'm suddenly feeling really motivated to squeeze my booty into some yoga pants, aren't you?

Of course, before you start any exercise program, but especially after you've just given birth, you should check with your doctor. There are actually some really good medical reasons for this—most noteworthy being that you can injure your already stretched and still-recovering abdominal muscles if you do too much, too soon. Plus, pregnancy can make your joints and ligaments all loosey-goosey, which means you won't be as coordinated as you were before you had your baby. Which in turn means you should probably hold off on the exercise class at the gym that requires you to hold a ten-pound weight while dancing to Belinda Carlisle until your baby is a few months old.

Once you get the final all-clear from your doc, you'll lose your best excuse to stay safely and comfortably on the couch and you'll have to start thinking creatively to come up with other excuses not to exercise. If you need some ideas, try, "I was up all night with the baby, so I'm going to have to use the small amount of energy I have to make it through the day." Or, "My old sports bra doesn't fit anymore, and the store had to special order me one in size 34H." Or, my personal favorite, "I'm finding that my baby is more fussy after I exercise. Must be all that lactic acid building up in my breast milk."

Anyway, eventually there comes a day when your motivation to lose the baby weight outweighs your motivation to stay on the couch. And on that day, the first thing you need to do is go to the athletic store and stock up on supercute athletic clothes. Of course, once that's done, you'll have to wash, fold, and dry all those clothes, so you'll unfortunately have to spend a couple more days on the couch. And once the required washing and folding are done, you may need to rewash and refold just to make sure everything is ready for your sporting debut. Then you may need a few days to prep yourself. Some time to do some warm-up stretches. A few days to pray. But once you're sure that you're ready, you'll get up. You'll lace on those tennies. You'll blast "Pump Up the Jam" on your iPod and then quickly swap it out for Hillsong when you realize it's too fast-paced. You'll fill up your water bottle. You'll go pee. And then you'll stand tall—and proud—because the time has (finally) come: you're going to get sporty.

Now, according to my personal-trainer friend Sarah, a new mom who is just restarting her exercise routine should start out with the goal of exercising for about thirty minutes at a time and do that between three and five times per week. If thirty minutes seems too long for you, you can break it up into ten-minute mini-jaunts throughout the day.

My only other piece of advice—besides just get out and do it—is to find yourself a workout partner. Nothing inspires me to get my booty off the couch like the threat of a big, fat, hormone-induced lecture about how I left my workout buddy alone with the crazy aerobics instructor. So find someone who has similar goals and join forces to hold each other accountable to exercise. I can say with a lot of confidence that if it weren't for Alisa—my half-marathon training partner, as well as my friend Rebecca, who forced me to get out and run with her twice a week for several months—I wouldn't have ever lost the baby weight.

Working Out with Baby

Now, before I go any further, I want to make sure to point out that your workouts aren't going to be anything like your pre-baby trips to the gym, when you spent an hour on the treadmill followed by a long, relaxing break in the steam room and a wheatgrass juice at the spa café. Because now you have a little one—a little one who gets hungry and tired and feels that twenty minutes at the gym is more than enough torture for one day. Okay, so maybe that's you. The good news is that there are lots of sporty things you can do with your baby in tow. Here are some ideas.

- **Take a mommy-and-me fitness class**. I love mommy-and-me fitness classes. There's just something about working out with a knowledgeable instructor in a group setting, combined with the fact that I'm super motivated not to be "that mom" who only does seven lunges when everyone else does eight, that makes for a great workout. And—if I'm being honest—it's actually kind of fun. Just don't tell anyone I said that.

- **Get a jogging stroller**. Let me just make this clear right off the bat: just because you have a jogging stroller, doesn't mean you have to jog. I hate jogging. But I love going on long walks with my girlfriends while pushing my babies in a jogging stroller. Of course, you can try to go on long walks with a regular stroller, but you'll spend more time trying to keep the wheels straight and the baby from being jostled than you will actually exercising.

- **Try exercises that can be done with baby**. Doing exercises with my baby is one of my favorite things to do—okay, one of my favorite sporty things to do. Here are a few to try:

  - Do lunges or squats with your baby strapped to your front in a Björn or other baby carrier. Talk about adding some extra resistance.
  - Get a baby backpack or front carrier and go on a hike.
  - Pop in an exercise video—Billy Blanks, anyone?—and let your baby watch your moves from the safety of an infant seat. Just make sure your baby is a safe distance away—I know how passionate some people get with their Tae Bo.
  - Lie on your back and lift your baby up and down, giving his little nose a kiss with each repetition. Or put him facedown on your knees and sing while you bounce him.

- **Join a gym**. I know gyms can be expensive—just last week, I calculated how many caramel macchiatos I could buy each month for the price of my gym membership, and that alone was enough to make me want to call in and cancel. But let me remind you of one thing—all those three-dollar lattes aren't helping you lose that baby weight or get healthier in any way. Your gym membership is. So if you find yourself struggling to find time or motivation to exercise, join a gym—preferably one with child care—and remind yourself how much cash you're paying every month for your membership. That always gets me going when I'm tempted to chill out on the couch instead of go to Pilates.

Your Final Motivational Send-Off

We're almost done. Now that I've motivated you to eat a little more healthily and (maybe) exercise, there's one final thing I have to warn you about: even if you manage to patiently and healthfully lose all the body weight, your body will never be the same. Growing a human inside yourself tends to change things. I told you earlier that I am (finally) down to my pre-pregnancy weight. What I didn't tell you is that I still have to wear a Spanx tank top every day because while the pounds are gone, the saggy skin on my belly is still there. And my hips are still wider. And my feet still have fat rolls. It's a bit irritating, but I'm finally reaching the place where I can admit that I'm okay with it. Because these are small sacrifices for the beautiful babies God gave me to carry. And, the truth is, while God does call us to take care of the bodies He gave us, He never called us to obsess over how our bodies look. What truly matters is how God sees us. And I can tell you with assurance that He couldn't care less about a few extra pounds or that leftover belly flab.

FIFTEEN

The Christian Daddy's Guide to Babies

What Dads Need to Know About Babies

Not to pull the "I-have-a-uterus" card out of my back pocket (again), but we moms go through a lot when raising our babies. And, well, let's just say that after a few weeks (plus) of bleary-eyed exhaustion, not to mention nine months of pregnancy or two years of adoption paperwork, most of us moms are ready for a little break. And even if it's just five minutes to pee without someone standing on your bladder, it's awfully nice to have Superdaddy-to-the-Rescue to swoop in, take that baby, and give a tired mama a break. Can I hear an amen, sisters?

Of course, as fantastic as Superdaddy is, there is a bit of a learning curve when it comes to taking care of a baby. And even if your husband is one of those guys who was raised with a gaggle of siblings and knows his way around a Diaper Genie like it's the back of his hand, he still will probably have a thing or two to learn when it comes to taking care of your baby. And that's where I come in.

I am (obviously) not a dad, so I can't give your husband the 411 on daddyhood. But I did the next best thing: I rounded up a group of been-there, done-that dads to give me the scoop on what they learned in their first year as a dad. They filled me in on their essential first-year learnings (eg, it's never a good idea to change a baby's diaper on your wife's white suede couch) and even shared some of their biggest failures and successes so that your husband, in turn, can truly step in and become your knight in shining armor and give you a few minutes' (or hours') break. And so, it's time for you to hand over the book to your hubby and kick back while he morphs into Superdaddy. Or at least a really great dad who knows exactly what to do with a screaming baby at three in the morning.

The Christian Daddy's Guide to Babies

First, let's meet our panelists:

Troy is not only a returning panelist and my baby brother, but his baby daddy skills are very fresh considering the fact that he has two daughters under two, along with a preschool-aged son. He's hoping that third time's the charm and that all the lessons he learned on babies #1 and #2 will serve him well during baby Elsie's first year.

Derek's parenting skills were proven when I asked his one-year-old son, Conner, what sound a giraffe makes and Conner confidently looked at me and sealed his mouth shut. Because giraffes don't make sounds. Talk about one smart kid. Or, as his parents say, "a hard worker." Either way, Conner is one of the most adorable, sweet, and precious kids I know, and I chalk that up—at least partially—to his amazing parents.

A.J. just started over being a baby daddy when his precious second son, Holden, arrived almost five years after his first son, Jacob. And while some parenting skills have had to be relearned, A.J. swears that it's just like riding a bike. Once you know, it all comes back fairly quickly.

Peter has a six-month-old son, Asa, with another baby on the way—meaning his two youngest will be less than a year apart. That's two in diapers. Two in bottles. Two in, well, just about everything. At least he won't have to worry about forgetting what parenting a baby is like.

Michael—whom you may recognize from my pregnancy book daddy panel—just became a daddy for the second time. This time with a sweet daughter, Emberly, who is just two years younger than her big brother, Caden. Which means Michael gets lots of baby-daddy practice—and has lots of middle-of-the-night time to contemplate the ins and outs of sleep training.

Here's what they think you—and your husband—need to know:

Troy on Playing with Babies

> *Baby Lesson #126: Babies aren't all that*
> *fun, but that's by God's design.*

I'll deny it if you ever tell my wife I said this, but my four-month-old daughter is a real bore. She really doesn't do anything fun. Not once in her short life has she cracked a hilarious kid joke or helped me build a mud spa for bugs in the backyard. In fact, even in her most exciting moments, a smile or a short giggle is about all I can get out of her.

For being the pinnacle of God's creation, you would think humans would be a little bit better off in the first year of life. I recently saw a video of a three-week old polar bear climbing up a steep, icy cliff. Horses, cows, deer—they can all walk within a few hours of birth. And lions, well, those cubs learn to hunt within their first few weeks of life. Frankly, I'm very disappointed in what my kids were capable of during the first months of life. Why did God ordain that human babies be so—dare I say—boring?

After giving this some thought, I have come to realize that perhaps our babies' dependency on us secures our relational bond. It's analogous to our relationship with Christ: if we were able to do everything in life confidently and perfectly from day one, I doubt we'd see a need for reliance on our Creator. Same with our kids. They need us to do, well, just about everything for them during the first year of life. But as we meet their needs, we're also showing them what Christ's love is all about.

And so, dads, even if your baby isn't your ultimate playmate (yet), do not miss out on these essential bonding months! Hold your baby often. Smile at, read to, and talk with him. Instead of wishing he could play I Spy with you, trust in God's good purposes in having him develop slowly, and enjoy the days when he will still snuggle with you. Because trust me: you will have plenty of opportunity in a few years to build pillow forts in the living room.

Derek on Free-Range Parenting

Baby Lesson #432: Sometimes it's okay to
let go of the rules and routines a little.

I've been trying to convince my wife to let me raise our son free-range. My initial plan was to purchase a couple of Border collies (or other "herding" dogs) and just put Conner in the backyard with the dogs and a couple of squeezie packs and let him run free every day. He could explore the yard, play and learn at his own pace, and curl up for a nap whenever he got tired. And, it seems like it would be fairly safe—I mean, if Conner got too near the water hose or started climbing the fence, the dogs would herd him back, right? But—imagine this—my wife put the kibosh on that before the idea ever even got off the ground.

But in all seriousness, I think there is something to be said for letting our babies have a little freedom to roam and explore. I'm not saying we should never schedule our kids or that we shouldn't have any rules, but simply that there is a time and a place for simply letting our kids *be*. I want to occasionally free Conner from a daily naps-at-nine, snack-at-ten schedule to give him time to explore and learn without structured learning activities or prepackaged educational games. To take him out of his safe-and-clean Pack 'n Play and let him get a little dirt under his nails. Just for a day or two.

I'm pretty sure my wife will go for that as long as I promise he'll be down for his nap at 9:30 sharp tomorrow. And that I do the herding instead of a pair of dogs.

Michael on Getting to Know Your Individual Children

*Baby Lesson #877: Spend time learning about
the way God created each of your children.*

Just when I thought I had my son, Caden, figured out, my daughter, Emberly, came along and threw me for a loop. You'd think that a baby is a baby is a baby. But no, the baby repertoire of sleeping, pooping, and eating looks different with each child. And so, all the tricks and tactics I learned with Caden didn't work with Emberly. I basically had to start over.

While calm words tended to stop Caden's tears, gentle rocking and snuggles helped Emberly. And while a sleep routine was exactly what Caden needed to start sleeping, Emberly needed dark and quiet in her room. And while silly faces and loud noise never failed to make Caden laugh, all that did for Emberly was make her break down in tears.

Interestingly, I found that the best way to learn about my kids' individual personalities is to spend time alone with each of them. When we are all together, I tend to respond to whichever kid is crying the loudest or laughing the most exuberantly. And in the midst of the chaos, it's hard to get a feel for their individual uniqueness. But when I make a pointed effort to spend time with them separately, I start to learn a bit about what makes them tick.

A few weeks ago, I took Emberly on a grocery-store excursion with me. I put her in the cart and pushed her around Fred Meyer.

I pointed out the colors of the fruits and the bright lights on the Christmas decorations, and she just beamed. I realized that while she's more reserved at home—probably as a result of her boisterous older brother's constant chatter—she's actually a kid who craves one-on-one attention. And so, I've made a mental note to spend alone time talking to her every day.

I think my biggest piece of advice for other dads is to take your baby away from everyone else—even their mommy—to get to know them a bit on an individual level. Even if it's a quick daddy-and-baby trip to the store or a walk around the neighborhood, that time will really help you bond with your baby and get to know him for the person God created him to be.

Peter on Midnight Feedings

Baby Lesson #987: Your wife probably does the brunt of the midnight feedings without you even knowing about it.

My six-month-old son, Asa, is adopted. Which means he's bottle-fed. Which means I can feed him just as easily as my wife can. Which means—as my wife has reminded me countless times—I am perfectly capable of taking over 50 percent of the feedings. You'd think this wouldn't be a comment-worthy revelation for a smart dad like me, but it was! My first daughter, Haddie, was breast-fed, which meant I blissfully slept through 90 percent of the midnight feedings, only waking up on the rare occasion that I valiantly decided to give my wife a break.

But with Asa, I was entirely capable of taking over at least half of the midnight feedings from day one. Which meant I had to drag my oblivious self out of bed every other night to give the little guy a bottle. After a week of that, I was exhausted! And then—surprise!—my wife got pregnant again. And since she was suffering from horrible morning sickness, I knew I needed to step up and do the big-dad thing and offer to do the midnight feedings every night.

Guys—I'm telling you—it was rough. The little dude cried at 2 a.m. for a bottle, and then sometimes again at 5 a.m. And on some nights, he woke up three or four times. One night I was up, trying to soothe him to sleep for—get this—five hours. Before long, I was a jittery, coffee-fueled, bleary-eyed mess. I asked my wife if this was normal—after all, she seemed to handle Haddie's early days with so much more grace and poise than I was—and she just smiled and said yes. Apparently most babies wake up multiple times at night. And most moms get up every night more than once to care for them. Every night. For months.

Dads, our wives are heroes! As some of you know, the midnight feedings, night after night, week after week, are incredibly exhausting and many of our wives manage them valiantly with nary a break for months. And so, if you can, offer to give your wife the occasional (or frequent) break, and make sure to tell her a big thank you. Because waking up for midnight feedings isn't as easy as it looks.

Troy on Milestones

> *Baby Lesson #1432: Act excited about your*
> *baby's accomplishments even if you're not.*

Apparently there is some sort of Internet class (or maybe it's a Facebook group?) that all women take on baby milestones. Because every mom I know is super enthralled by the time frame for when her baby should learn to smile, to laugh, to roll, and to burp. Just the other day, my wife was telling me all about how our daughter Elsie was right on track with her next milestone. I tried to listen and act interested—really—but after a while I just couldn't help but ask: "What's a milestone?"

It seems like every other minute, little Elsie is working on and then conquering another huge milestone. And regardless of my wife's (and my mom's) excitement, I have to wonder if all this hullaballoo is really that important. I mean, do we really need to take a hundred photos and send out a press release on the day my baby's nasty umbilical cord stub thing falls off? I mean, it's not like Elsie played a role in helping the thing shrivel up.

So, last week, when I walked in the door and my wife rushed to me and exclaimed "You'll never believe this! Elsie just scooched backward! She shouldn't be able to do that for two more weeks," I tried to put on my best proud-daddy face and act excited. But the truth is, all I saw was a baby lying on the ground. After staring for five minutes, I may have seen a slight twitch backward, but I'm not sure.

Anyway, I admit that I'm a bit underwhelmed by the milestones. I get that it's cool to see our babies learn and grow—but the truth is, these minor accomplishments are fairly routine. Like, I have yet to meet a baby who made it through his first year without losing his umbilical cord stub. But that said, our wives love stuff like that. They record it in their baby books and text all their friends and discuss it over lattes at the playground. I kid you not. And so, long story short, guys, be excited about the milestones your baby reaches, for your wife's sake. Because even if the smallest little scooch isn't important to you, it's important to her.

A.J. on the Necessary Equipment

Baby Lesson #2335: You may not have what it takes to be your baby's mom, but you have what it takes to be his dad.

I often feel very useless when it comes to parenting my sons. The truth is that they both prefer their mom—and rightfully so—she has all the necessary equipment to feed, nourish, and protect them. Just last week, I got home from work, and my wife handed my five-month-old over to me, and he immediately started crying. I rocked him; I snuggled him; I held him; I shushed him, to no avail. He wanted his mommy. And I was left feeling like the ultimate daddy failure.

But my sweet wife—after taking the baby and breast-feeding him into a state of calm—reminded me that I'm not Holden's mom. And that I wasn't built—physically or emotionally—to do the things a mom can do. And that's okay, because I'm a man—and while I'm an ultimate failure at all that "mom" stuff, I'm pretty darn good at doing all that "dad" stuff.

And so I've stopped trying to do "mom" things and started trying to do "dad" things with my sons. I sit on the couch with my sons and talk to them about sports and my stint in the army and about my latest workouts at the gym. I play catch—or in Holden's case, "roll." I love their mom—treating her with respect so they can learn what it means to lead a family. I've stopped trying to be something I'm not—and in the process, I've become much better at being the person I am.

The Christian Daddy's Guide to Babies, in Summary
(for Those Daddies Who Only Have Time to Read One Page)

- It's a bit of a bummer that your baby's UNO skills won't develop until he's about four—but that doesn't mean you shouldn't play with your baby.
- You weren't built to be a mom—physically or emotionally—so instead of trying to be like Mom, start trying to be a dad.
- Midnight feedings are rough. And your state of midnight oblivion doesn't do much to help your wife.
- Baby deer may be able to walk from day one—but your baby has them beat in the cuteness department.
- If your baby manages to move his finger while smiling, take a million pictures and rave to your wife about how advanced he is. Moms dig stuff like that.
- Take your baby out on "dates" away from other siblings and even mom, and get to know his unique personality.
- Really, you don't have the right equipment to be a mom. It's not worth even trying.
- Border collies do not make good babysitters. At least according to most women.

SIXTEEN

The Help-Daddy-Bond Initiative

Getting Close—and Staying Close—to Daddy

Before I had kids people kept warning me about how hard it would be to keep the romance alive in my marriage with kids underfoot. They warned me how exhausted I would be, how I'd never have time for my husband, and that even when I did have time, I'd be too tired to do anything about it. They warned me about how my hormones would soar and my sex drive would nose-dive and my husband would be put on the back burner as I dealt with diapers and feeding schedules and naps.

And I listened to every single thing they said and then quickly filed their sage words under "things to remember to lecture other people about when they get pregnant." Because none of it was going to happen to me. My marriage was different, and *we* were going to be just fine. No, better than fine. Our marriage was going to be even more intimate and more romantic than ever. We were going to be that couple that everyone else looked at with envy.

And that lasted about as long as it took for my husband to annoy me when I was in labor. So, about five minutes. Once we got home from the hospital, there was the occasional, "Let's just sit here on the couch and talk" that quickly turned into, "Let's just sit here on the couch and nap" and the frequent, "We'll get better about all this romance stuff once the baby is more self-sufficient." (Which, by the way, won't happen until either (a) he's gets married, or (b) you lose your grip on reality.) Anyway, we hadn't been home from the hospital for a week before our marriage had become everything that all the naysayers had warned us about.

Now, before I get into more details about the demise of our romance, I want to make one thing clear right off the bat: this was not my fault. I was pouring myself into our marriage, following every bit of well-meaning advice that anyone had ever given me about how to make my husband feel that he was still important. I can't remember the exact details, but I'm sure I spent a good ten minutes talking to him over the course of those first few weeks. And as if that weren't enough, I brought up all sorts of stimulating conversational topics—things like my need for sleep and the baby's pooping patterns—at least six times in every conversation. It really was a stellar effort on my part.

But—and this may come as a shock to you—all my hard work just wasn't enough. Things started to spiral. We drifted further and further apart until we reached a place where we hardly ever talked—and even when we did talk, it was about the baby and not about us. We never laughed. We never snuggled on the couch. We never had sex. The unthinkable happened: we became the people whom other people warn new parents about. We became a statistic.

All this thinking about statistics made me think about math, and thinking about math made me realize that something drastic had to be done to fix this—*stat*. Because anything that makes me seriously contemplate mathematics is obviously pretty dire. But out of my numbers-driven pain, an idea was born. An idea I like to call the Help-Daddy-Bond Initiative—an idea I think can help you overcome the your-marriage-is-doomed-because-you-have-a-baby phenomenon, but also can help you help your husband bond with your baby and be the spiritual leader God intended him to be. A tall order, I know, but you're a regular James Bond sort, aren't you?

Throughout the next few pages I'm going to challenge you to help your husband help himself—and in the process, help you save your marriage from the knowing smiles of all those people who filled your head with warnings about the demise of your marriage. And even more, these ideas will help you build a marriage that lives up to the standard for marriage that God has given us in the Bible. Because ultimately our goal has to be to serve Him through our lives, through our families, and through our marriages.

With that in mind, I've compiled a bunch of small things—we'll call them activities—you can do to help your husband bond with both you and your baby. Some of the things will help him bond with you. Others will help him bond with your family. And still others will help you bond as a family. Don't worry; I won't make you do something crazy, like have an in-depth conversation about your feelings or wear lingerie. At the beginning, at least. But every single one of these things will help get you on your way to having the marriage you want—and more important, the marriage God wants for you.

· ·

Time-Out for Mom

For When You're Praying for Your Husband

"I thank my God every time I remember you. In all my prayers for all of you, I always pray with joy because of your partnership in the gospel from the first day until now, being confident of this, that he who began a good work in you will carry it on to completion until the day of Christ Jesus." (Philippians 1:3–6)

Dear Lord, I thank You for my husband. I thank You for blessing me with a man that I am proud to raise my family with. I pray that You will fill his life with the peace and hope that comes from knowing You. Work in my husband's life, Lord! As he grows as a dad, help him also grow as a man, so the plan You have for his life will be fulfilled. Amen.

. . . .

Help-Daddy-Bond Activity #1: Help Daddy Bond with You

My marriage hit one of its lowest points right after our daughter, Kate, was born. We had two kids under two—which meant two kids in diapers who needed me 24/7 and one husband who certainly could understand that I was busy and tired and emotionally drained and certainly didn't have time to do time-consuming things like be nice to him. But it turns out that he was less understanding than I had expected. For some reason, he felt a bit neglected.

Anyway, right about that time, my friend read a book called *The Husband Project* (by Kathi Lipp). The gist of the book is that you do twenty-one little secret projects—things like making your husband a yummy dinner or buying him a surprise gift—all with the intention of making him feel loved and blessed and that your relationship with him is still a priority. My friend asked me to read the book and do the projects with her and be kind of like bless-your-hubby accountability partners.

At first I wasn't so sure about the idea. I was so, so tired. And I may have had a momentary meltdown when I realized that doing these projects added more stuff to my plate and didn't address the fact that I was totally emotionally spent and really didn't feel like doing nice things for anybody else—especially my husband. And I may have told myself that perhaps he should be doing nice things for me instead of me doing nice things for him. But I didn't say that stuff out loud. You know, because good Christian moms don't say stuff like that.

In the end I joined my friend in reading *The Husband Project*—not because I wanted to, but because God convicted me that it was the right thing to do. But the strangest thing happened: once I got going, I started to have fun with it. I actually liked doing nice things for my husband. It was addictive. I posted sticky notes on his mirror and bought him little treats and gave him free time when he wasn't expecting it. I even called his favorite pizza shop and had them deliver him his favorite pie at work. And he felt so special! And I loved that little tiny things—acts that took me fewer than five minutes to do—were making such a huge difference for him.

Also, just in case you're still wondering what's in it for you—I know I would be—this top-secret project actually helped me as well. Cam's attitude toward me grew softer. He felt loved and cherished and respected, so he was able to show me that he loved, cherished, and respected me as well. I really did go into it with the best intentions—to bless him—but it ended up blessing me as well.

Anyway, you don't have to do an elaborate project—although it is a lot of fun—to make your husband feel loved. But you do have to be intentional about it. And realize that while it feels a bit counterintuitive, one of the best things you can do for your relationship is to purposefully and intentionally treat your husband with the respect and care he deserves—that God has asked you to give him—whether you feel like it or not.

Help-Daddy-Bond Activity #2: Help Daddy Bond with You at Night—with Candles

The fact that your sex life has gone the way of *Dance, Dance Revolution* and disappeared since you had your baby actually has nothing to do with the fact that your neck is covered in spit-up and you have soggy Cheerios in your nursing bra. Nope, your post-baby sex-life decline comes down to one thing and one thing only: you're tired enough that if you have to choose between sex and sleep, you're going to choose sleep. Every single time.

But—just in case you've forgotten in your post-baby haze—sex is fun. And it's good for your marriage because it helps you feel all lovey-dovey with your husband. Which in turns makes you look at the world and your post-baby life with a smile-slapped-on-your-face glow. Sappy and romantic as it sounds, God blessed you with a husband who—lack of stain-removing knowledge notwithstanding—pretty much rocks. And that means you have to make building intimacy in your marriage a priority.

Ways to Increase Your Sex Life Without Totally Giving Up Your Sleep Life

1. **Do it with candles**. Set the mood—light a fire and open a bottle of wine or light some candles in your bedroom. Setting the scene will not only put you in the mood, but will also tell your husband that you're in the mood.

2. **Do it during your baby's nap**. Whoever said sex had to be a nighttime activity was obviously (a) a night person, and (b) a little bit drab. Because once you're a mom, you learn to get the stuff you have to get done when you have time to do it. And if that means having sex during your baby's nap, then have at it. Just be quiet, so you don't wake up the baby.

3. **Do it in the dark**. I'll go ahead and just speak for your husband for a second and tell you that he thinks you're a total hottie—stretch marks and extra baby weight and all. But I know what it's like to feel less-than-sexy post-baby. So, if you're more comfortable with the lights off, keep them off.

4. **Do it quickly**. You know what? I'm just going to come right out and say it: there is nothing wrong with the occasional

quickie. Kiss. Bond. Hug. Kiss again. And be asleep in time to get two hours of zzz's before the baby wakes up to nurse.

5. **Just do it**. Nike is onto something, because I have a sneaking suspicion that if you just have sex once or twice, you'll probably just want to do it again. Sometimes it just takes getting back on the horse to realize how much you like to ride. (Pun sort of intended.)

Help-Daddy-Bond Activity #3: Help Build Daddy's Confidence

Let me guess: Your husband doesn't do things the way you would like them to be done? For example, when you say, "Could you please give the baby a bath?" you mean, "Could you please take the baby upstairs, strip him down, run warm water in the tub, sing silly songs about fish to him while he plays, wash his hair with baby soap, dry him off, and then give him a culminating lotion massage before getting him dressed again? " But your husband hears, "Hey, take a baby wipe and wipe the baby's hands off."

Now, I admit that if that happened to me—not that I would know from experience or anything—I would probably say something sarcastic about how a baby wipe is not a bath and then grab the baby and go do it my way. But—get this—sarcasm and just doing things your way isn't good for your husband's daddy confidence. In fact, real research from real experts has shown that the more you criticize your hubby, the less likely he is to gain confidence in a skill. Which means that the more you criticize Daddy for taking care of the baby his way, the less likely he is to step up and help you take care of the baby. Talk about a catch-22.

But helping your husband to have confidence in his skills as a father actually helps your marriage. Not only does it help you to have someone else to change a diaper or do a midnight feeding, but also because the more time your husband spends bonding with your baby, the more confidence he'll get as a dad, as a husband, and as a man. And when your husband has more confidence in himself, your marriage will be stronger. It's kind of important.

So in order to help him build confidence (and in turn, bond with you and the baby), I want you to try something new. It's really easy. Basically, anytime your husband helps you with something baby-related and completes the task—even if he does it entirely differently than you would've done it—you're going to say, "Oh, wow! Nice job, honey!" and smile. And then leave it at that. No eye rolls. No why-can't-you-do-it-like-I-do-it? No grabbing the baby and redoing it. Just a deep, calming breath and then, "Oh, wow! Nice job, honey!"

Let's practice:

- Daddy just took the baby upstairs to get dressed, and she came down wearing a snowman sweater (it's July) and a swimsuit skirt.

  What do you say? *"Oh, wow! She looks great. Nice job, honey!"*

- Daddy took the baby on a little adventure so you could sleep in, and didn't come home until 11:30 a.m ... two hours after nap time should've started.

  What do you say? *"Oh, wow! Thanks for giving me so much time. Nice job, honey!"*

- Daddy went grocery shopping and came home with Froot Loops, coffee, and Hungry-Man frozen dinners. And that's it.

  What do you say? You guessed it: *"Oh, wow! You bought groceries! Nice job, honey!"*

Now, you might be thinking that all this praising and complimenting is going to backfire because you're going to end up with a husband who thinks Rice Krispies and string cheese is a four-star meal. But I think you may be surprised. Because if your husband is anything like mine (and I really hope he never, ever reads this, because then my secret strategy will be found out), he'll thrive on the compliments. And the more you compliment him, the more he'll want to please you. And chances are he's smart enough to figure out—eventually—that pleasing you means giving the baby a lotion massage after his tub bath.

Help-Daddy-Bond Activity #4: Help Daddy Bond with Baby

Don't tell my husband this, but I was a little irritated with him after my first baby was born because he seemed so indifferent. I mean, he loved Joey—no doubt—but he didn't seem to want to spend hours every day staring at him with awestruck eyes, wondering if God had ever created a baby quite as perfect or as beautiful. Cameron would do things like hold the baby while watching football. Or—get this— put him in the baby swing for a nap while he mowed the lawn.

I told my mom about how irritated I was and she sat me down and explained the facts of life to me: Women are the ones who carry and give birth to babies. And as we're doing all that carrying and birthing, we usually get all sentimental as we bond over the little kick-stretch codes that our babies use to communicate with us from the womb. So once those babies are born, we feel that we already know them. But daddy? Well, he has some catching up to do. And since you're such a helpmate (go you!), you may want to help him along a little.

But daddy will figure it out. By the time Joey was a few months old, Cameron was a regular bonding pro. He knew not only what made Joey laugh (him singing *catsandratsandelephants* while doing a little jig) but also what calmed Joey down when he was upset (also singing *catsandratsandelephants* while doing a little jig).

Your husband will get there. And here are some things you can do to help daddy and baby bond.

1. **Send daddy to read**. Here's a little hint: your newborn couldn't care less about whether the three little pigs find a safe place to live. In fact, most likely, he's not even listening to the words in the story, but instead, just to the cadence of your hubby's voice. This is good news (for now)—because now your husband can toss aside *The Three Little Piggies* and bond with your baby over the NBA play-offs round-up in *Sports Illustrated*. And if that's not motivation for your hubby to bond, I don't know what is.

2. **Encourage daddy to hone in on his talents**. I'm not going to name any names, but there's a certain daddy I know who can rock out to the Pajama Jams like no other. He does this little hip-swing thing and this silly little voice, and let's just say that it can make kids—and moms—of all ages dissolve into a fit of laughter. Encourage your hubby to be "that guy" with your baby and to develop his ability to sing "Jesus Loves Me" like an aardvark or to impersonate VeggieTales as he tucks the baby into bed. Your baby may not appreciate it now, but by the time he turns one, I can guarantee he'll he begging for Mr. Tomato to come tuck him in.

3. **Give daddy the facts**. Many men like concrete, mathematical facts—which explains why I'm known as the "man whisperer" in many circles. Okay, so I've never actually been called that, but I did figure out that the best way to gently encourage my hubby to do something parent-ish was to give him research-proven facts to demonstrate why doing things like reading or singing or diaper changing is good for babies. So when I explained to him that babies who had skin-to-skin contact with their parents had something like a 324 percent chance of being more social when they grew up (as you can see, I'm very good with my calculations), my husband jumped right on board with the kangaroo care idea and

started spending time every day snuggling skin to skin with Joey.

4. **Take pictures**. Okay, so I know you're already taking, like, a bazillion pictures of your baby every day. But today, try doing a little photo shoot of baby and daddy together. Not only will you have some great shots to send to your mother-in-law (which, by the way, will score you major daughter-in-law points), but you'll also be able to show your hubby how great he's doing as a daddy.

8 Things You May Need to Help Daddy Bond

1. A diaper bag that he's not embarrassed to carry. And yes, that means that the turtles–'n'-froggies diaper bag that was just too cute not to buy has got to go. But you knew that anyway, didn't you?
2. A toothbrush.
3. Lingerie.
4. A good attitude. (Say it with me again, just for good measure: *"Oh, wow! Nice job, honey!"*)
5. A camera to capture all those supersweet moments that you have as a family.
6. Candles. And Norah Jones playing on your iPad.
7. A monthlong supply of man food (chocolate chips, tortilla chips, and hamburger should do it) so you can cook your man a nice dinner as he bonds.
8. An iPad. (Okay, so you don't really need an iPad to help daddy bond per se, but it will definitely make your downtime more fun, which in turn makes you more fun, which in turn means, well, you get the picture.)

Epilogue

A Sappy Dissertation from a Toddler's Mom

My son Will just blew out the candles on his first birthday cupcake last night. Okay, he tried to grab the fire, and I quickly blew out the flame before he got burned, but you get the idea. My baby is one. And I have a whole pile of clothes covered in chocolate frosting to prove it.

As you know, Will is my third baby. And while I went all out for Joey's first birthday, hiring a pastry chef to make him a Hungry Caterpillar cake and hosting a huge first birthday bash in our backyard so everyone could see him smear frosting all over his face, Will just had a small party. Or maybe I should call it a gathering. Or, a family dinner where we happened to serve cake and dig an old birthday candle (probably left over from Joey's first birthday) out of our pantry so we could sing.

It's not that I love Will any less—he's fantastic—but simply that I have changed so much in the six years since I became a mother. And the old Erin—the one who had the mental capacity to plan a party—has disappeared along with my pink ballet flats (they are now "princess shoes") and my skinny jeans (I finally had to just let that dream go). Because motherhood has changed me. To the core.

There are days when I'm not sure I like the "new Erin." There are days I feel nostalgic for the way things used to be—when my house was spotless, when I had a healthy dinner waiting for my husband every night when he came home, when I had time to paint my nails, to read about theology, and to go out for coffee with my friends. But then I glance up and see a picture of my kids hanging on the wall in my cluttered living room, and reality hits. Yes, things were simpler before I became a mom. But not better. And certainly not happier.

Because—and you'll have to indulge me while I get all sentimental on you—I have no doubt that when God created me, He created me for a purpose. And one of those purposes is raising my precious and wonderful babies up to love and serve Him. God has given me the chance to show my sons—my strong, energetic, and passionate Joey, and my hilarious, outgoing, and curious Will—how He created them to be courageous leaders and warriors for Him. And God has blessed me with a daughter—my smart, tender, and creative Kate—and commissioned me to teach her about His calling in her life. No wonder motherhood has changed me.

It's ironic that right as I'm finishing this book, my youngest is also finishing up his first year of life. Unless God has another surprise in store for me, I'm done having babies. I'm done with those up-all-night sessions in the baby rocker and with trying to find a quiet (and private) place to breast-feed in public. I'm done with Baby Björns and Nap Nannies and baby gyms. I'm done with bruises on my leg from trying to carry the infant carrier into the house. Done. And while it's exciting to be looking forward to what's still to come—to seeing my kids' personalities emerge, their faiths solidify, their love grow—it's also bittersweet. Because—and now I'm going to start crying—God gives us such a short time with these precious little souls. And I'm amazed at how quickly a year can fly by—especially when that last hour before daddy comes home every afternoon seems to take an eternity.

So, as I OxiClean that chocolate frosting out of Will's birthday outfit, I'm going to be grateful. Grateful that I have a shirt to scrub. Grateful for Will's exuberance and energy and laughter. Grateful that I have these happy-yet-bittersweet memories to treasure, even as I struggle to figure it all out. Because God has blessed me with these precious children. And I'm not sure He could've given me a better gift.

About the Author

Erin MacPherson is a mom of three who wants to come beside her readers not only as a confidante and Christian sister, but also as a friend who understands what it's like to juggle kids, life, and a much-too-messy house. When she discovered she was pregnant she decided to write about it—but then kept writing. A former staff writer and editor for Nickelodeon, Erin now entertains parents on her personal blog, www.christianmamasguide.com, as well as through her staff writing job with WeAreTeachers.com, freelance magazine articles, devotionals and speaking. Erin, her assistant principal husband Cameron, and her kids Joey (7), Kate (5), and Will (1) live in Austin, Texas.

To my Christian mama friends:

Congrats on your first year of motherhood! I'm so glad we were able to take this journey together and I pray that your transition is full of tender and sweet moments.

I would love to hear more about you—and of course, your baby. Please drop by my website at www.christianmamasguide.com or e-mail me at erin@christianmamasguide.com. I can't wait to get to know you better!

Blessings,
Erin

Index

breast pump, 29, 74–75, 88–89

breast-feeding, 65–83
>   FAQs, 81–83
>   the first two weeks, 71–75
>   fluids and, 72
>   gear, 73–75
>   productive things to do while, 75–77
>   in public, 78–79
>   reasons to breastfeed, 66–68
>   reasons not to breastfeed, 68–70

C

cabbage leaves (for breast engorgement), 29, 80

calming techniques (to encourage infant sleep), 56

car seat, 54, 109, 114, 144–45

CareCalendar (www.carecalendar.org), 4

catheter, 17

Christian moms, what makes us different, 7

churches, as activity sources, 152

cloth diapers, 99–100

coffee, 62

colds and runny noses, 124–25

colic, 126

convertible car seat, 114–15

cradle cap, 42

croup, 126

C-section
>   healing, 18–19
>   tips to help you heal after a, 19–20

D

daddy: advice from a
>   on baby's milestones, 201–2
>   on free-range parenting, 198–99
>   on getting to know your individual children, 199–200
>   on midnight feedings, 200–1
>   on the necessary equipment (for being a dad), 202–3
>   on playing with babies, 197–98

depression (postpartum), 23

Desitin, 102

diaper rash, 99, 101–2, 166

diapering, 95–107
>   advanced diapering moves, 106–7
>   mastery of the art of, 106–7
>   three basic rules for effective, 104–6

diapers
>   choosing the right, 97–101
>   saving money on, 103–4

diarrhea, 125, 128, 159

diet (for postpartum weight loss), 188–90

dietitian, feeding advice from a registered, 155–69

disposable diapers, 98–99

drooling, 42

Dusan, Alisa (registered dietitian), feeding advice from, 155–69

E

E.A.S.Y pattern, 58

ear infections, 124

eating to lose the baby weight, 188–90

emergency room trip versus call to doctor, 127–29

engorgement, 28–30

episiotomy, 14

ER trips, 127–28

exercising
>   to lose the baby weight, 190–92
>   with baby, 192–94

ExerSaucer, 114, 135

F

feeding advice from a registered dietitian, 155–69

Ferber, Richard, 58–59

Ferberizing, 50, 58

fever, 125, 128

finger foods, 162–63

fingernails and toenails (newborn), 42–43

fluids and breast-feeding, 72

food (solid),
    finger foods, 162–63
    making your own, 160–62
    when to start your baby on, 156–57
    your baby feeding plan, 157–60
food allergies, 165–66
foreplay, 32–33
formula
    basics, 90–92
    preparing and storing, 91–92
front carrier, 193

G

G-diapers, 100–1
gear. *See* baby gear; sleep gear; breast-
feeding (gear),
going out with baby checklist, 144–45
guilt (the "mommy guilts"), 175–76

H

Happiest Baby on the Block, The (Karp),
56
Healthy Sleep Habits, Happy Child
(Weissbluth), 56
heart medications and breast-feeding,
70
Help-Daddy-Bond Initiative, the, 206
    activities to help Daddy bond with
    baby and you, 208–15
    8 things you may need to help
    Daddy bond, 215
high chair, 112–13
hormones, postpartum flood of, 21–22
hydration, 20, 72

J–K

jaundice, 126–27
Jesus
    activities that will teach your baby
    about, 138–39
    age-appropriate books that will
    teach your baby about Jesus,
    139–40
    how to teach babies about, 8–9
jogging stroller, 114, 193

Karp, Harvey, 56

L

Lansinoh, 27
Lansinoh Soothies, 28
light, and baby's sleep, 53–54
lochia, 20–21
losing the baby weight, 185–94
Lotrimin AF, 102
lubricant (personal), 33
lullaby CD, 61
lying-in period, 11–34

M

Mama Needs a Time-Out (Riggleman),
177–78
mealtime, Christian mama's mini
guide to, 167–68
Medela Pump In Style, 75
medications
    and breast-feeding, 70
    for PPD, 23
midnight feedings, a dad's thoughts on,
200–1
mini-breaks
    for mom and baby, twenty, 180–81
    for you, twenty, 182–83
Mommy & Me classes, 150–53
monitor (baby), 113
mood swings, 22, 187
MOPS (Mothers of Preschoolers),
145–46
    10 things learned at, 146
Mothers of Preschoolers. *See* MOPS
music
    to calm your baby, 40
    to calm yourself, 178
    to get baby to sleep, 54, 61
    to help you make time for God, 178

N–O

nap nanny, 60
new mom groove, how to get into the,
2–5

spiritual time-out, 176–78
spitting up, 41
stool softeners, 15–16
stroller, 112, 114, 193
swaddler, 61
swaddling (to encourage infant sleep), 56, 61
swaddling wrap, 110
swing (baby), 40, 110–11

T-U-V

taking care of you, 171–83
teaching babies about Jesus, 8–9, 138–40
thrush, 125
time-out
    spiritual, 176–78
    taking a, 173–74
    a working mommy, 179–81
toilet
    first trip to (postpartum), 16
    five things you need to know about post-childbirth trips to the, 17–18
toys for baby, 113–14, 135–37

umbilical cord, 44

vaccines, 123–24
vaginal dryness, 33
Velcro swaddler, 61
Vicodin (for postpartum pain), 15
video camera, 111–12
video monitor, 113
vomiting, 41, 125, 128, 129, 159

W-Y

waiting room (at the pediatrician's office), 119–20
water (for postpartum healing), 16, 20
weaning, 29, 79–80
weighing (baby), 120–21
weight loss, postpartum, 185–94
Weissbluth, Marc, 51, 56
well check, 121–24
West, Kim, 51
white noise, 40, 53, 61
wipes
    choosing the right, 102–3
    saving money on, 103–4
working out with baby, 192–94
WubbaNub, 111

YMCA, 152